*The Wo...
Ultimate Cocktail Book*

# The Wordsworth
# *Ultimate*
# *Cocktail Book*

—

*Ned Halley*

**Wordsworth Reference**

The edition published 1998 by Wordsworth Editions Ltd
Cumberland House, Crib Street, Ware, Hertfordshire SG12 9ET

Text copyright © Ned Halley

Wordsworth® is a registered trade mark of
Wordsworth Editions Ltd

ISBN 1 85326 762 7

Typeset by Antony Gray
Printed and bound in Great Britain by
Mackays of Chatham plc, Chatham, Kent

*For Max & Lydia*

# Contents

# Author's Note

I have been collecting cocktail recipes for a long time. It's a process I have accelerated of late in the quest to find at least a thousand distinct concoctions for this book.

Because I write about the pleasures (and occasionally the perils) of drinking strong liquors in my magazine *Spyglass* and elsewhere, I have many opportunities to ask people for their own recipes. And just about everyone does, indeed, seem to have a favourite. So it has not been a great struggle to exceed my target by a long shot.

I am very grateful to all those who have contributed their own peculiar mixtures to the following pages. There have been many nominations of the same cocktails, of course, and I have discovered that there are very different versions even of the classic recipes. The ingredients may differ, but more often it's the proportions. The established guides to the subject, such as *The Savoy Cocktail Book* and *America's International Bartender's Guide* demonstrate clearly just how arbitrary the ingredient mix can be.

Take the classic brandy-based Sidecar. I have found recipes directing the use of equal proportions of brandy, Cointreau and lemon juice; and recipes employing two parts brandy to one each of Cointreau and lemon juice – and recipes for equal amounts of the spirits and just a teaspoon of lemon juice. All Sidecars, but all very different drinks.

The versions of these classic cocktails in this book are those I, and my long-suffering co-researchers, have judged, as best we can, to be the best – after rigorous hours of experimentation with bottles and shaker. Naturally, tastes differ, so it is axiomatic that users of this book should feel free to adjust any of the recipes according to their own preferences.

Everyone asks if I have tested *all* the cocktails in the process of concocting this book. The answer is yes – and no. Many of the recipes are ones I have tried over the years and have felt no urge to reprise. And many more are variations on a core theme with which I am familiar but not in a position to test item by item. I will go so far as to say that none of the cocktails in this book has seemed to me too revolting to drink, but a few concoctions I have tried – particularly those involving the new generation of sweetened and coloured liqueurs – have been quite firmly left out.

If there is one category of cocktails I have deliberately overlooked, it is those which depend on the use of food mixers, liquidisers or other electrical kitchen-processing equipment. Almost all the recipes in the book can be made with the aid of no utensil more complicated than a shaker and strainer. I believe the best cocktails are made with simple ingredients and simple implements.

This is a particularly good time in the two-century history of the cocktail to be collecting recipes, because we are now in the midst of a vigorous cocktail renaissance. Chic bars, clubs and restaurants have been flourishing and multiplying throughout the 1990s, and manufacturers worldwide have introduced dozens of new and mixable branded drinks to tempt adventurous consumers.

Cocktails have not always been in fashion. They were popular 100 years ago, in the Naughty Nineties and for the opening years of this century, on both sides of the Atlantic. But the First World War ended the craze. Cocktails revived in the roaring twenties – when they were found to be ideal camouflage for the bootleg spirits so relished in the midst of America's Prohibition – but lost ground to the austerity of the Depression before being extinguished by the Second World War.

Urged on by a trend-obsessed media and the lavish advertising campaigns of the liquor producers, today's cocktail craze must represent the greatest boom in the history of mixed drinks. In the last bull market, between the world wars, these confections were the exclusive preserve of what might legitimately be called the cocktail society – in other words, the rich.

But today, every bar and bistro, pub and club seems to have cocktails to hand – even if only in the form of ready-mixed drinks mass-produced under famous brand names such as Bacardi, Gordon's or Smirnoff. And while not so long ago you had to brave the swishy cocktail bars of the Plaza or the Savoy to find a perfect martini, or a bartender who knew the difference between a Manhattan and a Margarita, you'll now find proficient shakers and stirrers on call in even the most modestly pretentious city watering holes of Europe and America.

The intention of this book is simply to offer practical advice to cocktail aspirants whose thirsts have been whetted by the current craze. Making cocktails at home is enormous fun, and very much easier than some bartenders make it seem. All you need is a shaker, a few essential ingredients – and the urge to experiment.

# Introduction

The young drinkers sipping piña coladas and brandy sours in fashionable city bars throughout the world today may well believe that the cocktail is an invention of their own time. But the present vogue for colourful alcoholic concoctions is no more than the latest chapter in a two-hundred-year history.

It all began in the newly independent United States of the late 1700s. The first 'definition' of the word cocktail is possibly that given in the 1801–08 edition of New York's *Columbian Repository*: 'a stimulating liquor composed of spirits of any kind, sugar, water and bitters.'

As descriptions of cocktails go, it has probably never been bettered. As to the word itself, the likeliest source is a drink in which the spoon used to stir the mixture is left in the glass. At American horseracing courses two centuries ago, it was common for punters to watch the races while holding a glass of spirit mixed with water or fruit juice. The spoon (or other implement) was retained to give the mix an occasional stir. The story goes that the projecting spoon reminded equestrian enthusiasts of the upright, docked tails of mixed-bred hunters and draught horses, as distinct from thoroughbred racehorses. 'Cocktailed' is still a common description in the US for a non-thoroughbred animal.

There are countless other suggested origins, including claims that the cocktail was an invention of American barkeeper Betsy Flanagan, and that the name follows that of an Aztec princess called Coctel. Allusions to poultry feathers seem wide of the mark. Likelier is some connection with a wine-based drink from Bordeaux long known as the *coquetel*.

Whatever the case, the word is firmly established in everyday language – and not just in the context of mixing drinks. In the loose-knit lingo of fashion, a cocktail frock is a shorter version of an evening frock. A cocktail party is one to which most of the guests are expected to leave before dinner. And politicians of all parties have long been accustomed to having their sincerest pronouncements branded 'a cocktail of deceits and half-truths.'

The cocktail may wax and wane in popularity, but it looks set to be with us for a century or two yet. And so to the twin purposes of this book: to provide more recipes than have ever previously appeared in one volume, and to make their preparation as simple as possible for the enthusiastic amateur.

Making cocktails at home, the obvious limitation is the number of ingredients to hand. That's why this book is arranged in sections according to prinicipal ingredients – individual spirits, liqueurs and wines. Where a single ingredient dominates – usually because it is the only spirit, or the one used in the greatest quantity – the cocktail appears under the heading of that spirit. Thus a cocktail comprising two parts gin and one part rum will be found under Gin. Where two or more principal ingredients figure equally, the cocktail frequently appears under each of the appropriate headings. Thus, a cocktail composed of one part gin and one part rum will be found under both Gin and Rum.

Because some ingredients, such as individual liqueurs, don't have their own headings, the glossary/index at the end of this book gives references to all the cocktails in which these products are included. So, if you have, say, a bottle of Grand Marnier and would like to know which recipes utilise it, simply look up the name in the glossary and you will find a list of cocktails, and the headings under which they appear.

## The Vital Ingredients

You'll need a basic collection of essential drinks to enable you to make a reasonable variety of cocktails on the spot. These include brandy, gin, rum and some kind of whisky as principal ingredients. You should also keep dry and sweet vermouth, Cointreau, apple brandy and pastis. Bénédictine, Campari, Chartreuse, curaçao and Dubonnet all crop up frequently. Cream liqueurs, particularly crème de cacao and crème de menthe, are useful.

Angostura bitters are a *sine qua non*, and orange bitters likewise. Among non-alcoholic items, grenadine is vital. Fruit juices are indispensable, so keep a constant supply of fresh fruit for squeezing, or cartons for opening. One of the quirks of the recipes in this book is that lime juice is always specified as *fresh* lime juice – a sanction not similarly applied to lemon, orange or other juices. The intention is to provide a constant reminder that the recipe calls for the juice of the lime and **not** for lime juice cordial – an excellent product, but a very different thing from the juice of the fruit.

All the ingredients mentioned throughout the book are described in brief in the glossary on pages 287–96.

## Equipment

The one irreplaceable item is a good cocktail shaker. It should be an unadorned model with a capacity of a pint (0.5 litre) or more. The simplest to use is the type with a lid incorporating the strainer. The main lid is removed to allow the ice and ingredients to be added and, after shaking, a lid-within-the-lid is detached to effect pouring through a perforated section. If you prefer the more basic model, you will need a good strainer which will fit closely within the mouth of the shaker for pouring.

Some cocktails call for the use of a food mixer or blender. On the whole, these recipes are excluded from this book, because the protracted ritual of using and then cleaning a blender seems to run contrary to the whole spirit of making cocktails. If these drinks aren't easy, they aren't fun.

Otherwise, the necessary equipment should already be to hand in the kitchen.

## Glasses

The 'traditional' cocktail glass is a familiar icon – a shallow cone-shaped bowl connected by a stem to a circular base. This classic shape, considered *de rigueur* for a martini, comes in different sizes and widely varying qualities. Size is a matter of choice, but quality is worth paying for. Choose a maker whose glass is fine and uncut and has a rim that comes to a thin, polished finish. Cheap glasses with a thick, rolled rim are much less of a pleasure to drink from, and to look at.

That said, cocktails can be drunk with equal pleasure from small brandy or wine glasses – or any stemmed glass that holds about the right amount, and is pleasing to the eye. Colour is an important element in many recipes, so choose plain, uncut and untinted glassware. Tumblers and tall 'highball' glasses should be chosen with the same criteria in mind.

## Measures

Cocktail recipes are commonly measured in fluid ounces. In bars, measures of spirit were once commonly served in proportions of gills – a quarter, a fifth or a sixth – but these arcane rations are gradually disappearing. In Europe, metrication has introduced two standard spirit measures of 25 and 35 milliltres (ml) for use in bars. These equate very roughly to an ounce and an ounce and a half. More exactly, a bar serving these standard measures can calculate that it will get 28 'single' measures each of 25ml from a standard (70cl) bottle of spirits.

For home cocktail mixers, an ounce or 25ml makes a logical unit. But these quantities become hard to follow when recipes express them as fractions or decimals. Thus, a list of ingredients might look like this:

| 1½ fl. oz dry gin | *or, even sillier:* | 37.5ml dry gin |
| ¾ fl. oz Dubonnet | | 18.75ml Dubonnet |
| ½ fl. oz Campari | | 12.5ml Campari |

This seems to make the whole thing look unnecessarily daunting, especially for those who find fractions and decimals difficult at the best of times. So, in this book, such arithmetical headaches are avoided. Ingredients are expressed in units, symbolised by a measuring cup – ╏ – and the differing proportions are conveyed via an appropriate number of cups.

So, the recipe above is expressed as:

╏ ╏ ╏ dry gin
╏ ╏ Dubonnet
╏ Campari.

Now the point is not to encourage enthusiasts to mix single-serving cocktails comprising six measures of alcohol. It is to provide an immediately obvious guide to the relative quantities of the ingredients. The secret of a good cocktail is the balance of those ingredients. The size of measure you use is entirely your choice, according to how many people you're making the drink for, and how thirsty they are. The recipe above, using a one-ounce measure, would make two generous cocktails or, obviously, one generous cocktail if a half-ounce measure is employed.

If you make cocktails regularly, you should acquire one or more standard measuring cups – say, one of one ounce and one of half an ounce. Bear in mind that a fluid ounce equates to about two tablespoonfuls of liquid. In kitchenware and hardware shops, you should be able to find purpose-made measuring cups. The best are of the hour-glass shape adopted for the symbol used in this book. The standard version of these double cups has a one-ounce measure one end and a one-and-a-half-ounce measure at the other. Alternatively, make use of a liqueur glass or any other adaptable vessel.

The other liquid measure (besides the self-evident teaspoon) used in this book is the 'dash'. This is taken to be three or four drops – as in a dash of Angostura bitters. Numerous recipes call for two, or three or four dashes of one or more supplementary ingredients. The recipes in this book work on the unashamedly random reckoning that six or seven dashes are equal to about a teaspoonful.

Recipes for punches and other bulk mixes are simplified as much as possible in measurement terms. A 'bottle' of spirits is taken to be the standard size of around 24–25 fluid ounces or 70 centilitres (also known as a 'fifth' in the US, as in a fifth of a gallon). A bottle of wine is based on the worldwide standard of 75cl. Measurements of other drinks in bigger quantities, such as fruit juices, are given in both imperial (pints) and metric (litres) with equivalents based on the very simplified basis of one pint to half a litre.

## Methods

Cocktails are either shaken or stirred. The difference is simple enough. A shaken cocktail comes out cloudy, and probably with a suspension of tiny fragments of ice that have managed to infiltrate the strainer. Stirred cocktails are clear.

Both styles share the essential condition of being cold. Shaking and stirring are intended not just to mix the ingredients, but to chill them. As a rule, recipes including sliced whole fruit or fruit juices, milk or cream, sugar or syrups are shaken. They would be cloudy even if stirred, and shaking does a better job of mixing them anyway.

A skilled mixer ensures that the ingredients are in contact with the ice for as short a time as possible. This is simply because ice melts rapidly, and wateriness is the ruin of any cocktail. So, when mixing drinks that have more than a couple of ingredients, it makes sense to combine all of them in one container before preparing the shaker or stirring jug. Purists refrigerate all the ingredients in advance.

Take the ice from the freezer only when you are ready to shake or stir. The ice should fill about one third of the shaker's capacity and likewise in a stirring jug. Add the ingredients immediately.

A vigorous shake of about 10 to 20 seconds should do nicely, and the contents must be dispensed at once. If there is any mix remaining in the shaker, strain it off the ice into another container – otherwise when you come back for seconds, the cocktail will be largely water.

Stirring is a more delicate art. Again, it's vital to keep the ingredients in contact with the ice for the minimum possible time, but it's equally important to mix and chill the components thoroughly. Use a long metal spoon to whizz the ice around vigorously for 20 seconds or so, and strain the drink off as soon as stirring is complete. As with shaking, don't leave any residue in the jug with the ice. Remove the ice and refrigerate the jug for later.

If it troubles you that the melting ice inevitably imparts a little water into your drink during the shaking or stirring process, you might consider investing in some of the patent cubes or balls which contain a quantity of water sealed within. These are frozen and used in the normal way, but of course don't leak any water into the mix. They must, of course, be washed and dried before replacing in the freezing compartment.

Ice Cube of Sweden make an interesting variation on the frozen-water theme. Their standard-sized cubes are made from soapstone. Kept in the freezer they act just like ice cubes, but have the twin merits of not diluting your cocktail, and of being eternally reusable. The stone, treasured by the Vikings for its heat-retaining properties, is quarried from deposits estimated to be 400 million years old.

Enthusiasts who don't wish to employ any kind of ice in the chilling and mixing process keep all the components in the fridge or freezer.

Thus, a very dry martini can be made simply by putting a drop or two of chilled dry vermouth into a cocktail glass and topping up with gin straight from the freezing compartment. Spirits will remain fluid in all but the frostiest freezers, but will take on a temporary oily weightiness which you may or may not find appealing.

Some cocktail enthusiasts like to refrigerate their glasses. This certainly helps keep the drinks cold, and produces a picturesque frosting effect on the glass if the fridge is cold enough. But it makes the stem slippery – so beware.

Garnishes and decorations on cocktails are a topic of much trivial dispute. Snobs consider it *de trop* to add anything to a classic drink other than the merest whiff of essential oils from a delicately manipulated citrus peel. Less-inhibited drinkers, on the other hand, feel that a cocktail just isn't worthy of the name unless it looks as colourful and garlanded as possible.

The recipes in this book include fruits and other extras only where they add quite specifically to the flavour, rather than the appearance, of the cocktail. But if you wish to decorate any drink with cocktail-stick umbrellas, brochettes of sliced fruit and garden blooms, then garnish away at will.

# ANIS & PASTIS

Heirs to absinthe, the allegedly lethal *digestif* that was proscribed under French law in 1915, anis and pastis are the aniseed-flavoured apéritif spirits that turn to a milky opacity when mixed with water. Just as absinthe was a popular ingredient in cocktails a century ago, so are its successors today. The name absinthe is nostalgically retained in many of the items in this section, perhaps in anticipation of the day when the old wormwood-based original will once again be licensed for sale.

Famous brands such as Pastis 51, Pernod and Ricard will all do very well for the recipes below. At a pinch, the pastis of Greece, ouzo (or the raki of Turkey), can be substituted for the French brands.

## Absinthe

- pastis
- water

dash Angostura bitters

dash sugar syrup

*Shake over ice until almost frozen. Strain into a cocktail glass and add a lemon peel twist.*

*An 'Absinthe American' is a sweeter version. Simply add two or three extra dashes of sugar syrup.*

## Absinthe Cooler

- whisky

teaspoon lemon juice

dash Angostura bitters

pastis

ginger ale

*Stir first three ingredients in a tall glass with ice. Top up with ginger ale and a dash or two of pastis.*

## Absinthe Drip

**⚡** pastis

sugar lump

iced water

*Pour pastis into a small glass, hold the sugar lump on a perforated drip spoon (or other strainer). Drip iced water on to the lump to dissolve the sugar into the drink.*

## Absinthe Frappé

**⚡⚡** pastis

**⚡** Anisette

**⚡⚡⚡** water

*Shake over ice until almost frozen. Strain into a cocktail glass.*

## Absinthe Friend

**⚡** pastis

**⚡** dry gin

dash Angostura bitters

dash sugar syrup

*Shake over ice. Strain into a cocktail glass.*

## Atom Bomb

**⚡** pastis

**⚡** brandy

*Stir over ice. Strain into a cocktail glass.*

## Brunelle

**⚡** pastis

**⚡⚡⚡** lemon juice

teaspoon sugar

*Shake over ice. Strain into a cocktail glass.*

Edgar Degas' immortal portrait of Paris low-life, *Absinthe*, features a young woman seated in melancholy contemplation of a glass of the notorious green wormwood liquor. The model is commonly believed to have been a prostitute, but was in fact an unwitting Ellen Andrée, a well-known actress and mannequin for the fashion house Worth, who appears in many of Manet's and Renoir's most glamorous café scenes. When she found out about *Absinthe*, she was furious with Degas, and accused him of 'massacring' her reputation, if only because no respectable member of Paris society was ever seen to drink absinthe.

## Duchess

- pastis
- dry vermouth
- sweet vermouth

*Stir over ice. Strain into a cocktail glass.*

## Earthquake

- pastis
- bourbon
- gin

*Stir over ice. Strain into a sherry or cocktail glass.*

## Esther Rantzen

- Pernod
- ouzo

teaspoon marmalade

salt

*Wet the rim of a cocktail glass and dip into salt to encrust. Add ingredients to glass.*

*Device of Adrian Edmondson and Rik Mayall for BBC TV's cult comedy* Bottom, *so-named after the dentigerous eponymous television presenter because the drink 'pulls yer gums back over yer teeth.'*

## Gasper

- pastis
- gin

*Stir over ice. Strain into a cocktail glass.*

## Glad Eye

- pastis
- peppermint cordial

*Stir over ice. Strain into a cocktail glass.*

## Macaroni

- pastis
- sweet vermouth

*Stir over ice. Strain into a cocktail glass.*

The first absinthe factory was opened in Switzerland in 1797 by Henri Dubied, who sold the spirit as an aphrodisiac. Dubied's son-in-law, Henri-Louis Pernod, followed him into the business, starting production in France in 1805.

## Nine-Pick

**❚❚** pastis

**❚** gin

dash Angostura bitters

dash orange bitters

dash sugar syrup

*Shake over ice. Strain into a cocktail glass.*

## Pansy

**❚❚** pastis

**❚** grenadine

dash Angostura bitters

*Stir over ice. Strain into a cocktail glass.*

## Pansy Blossom

**❚❚** pastis

teaspoon grenadine

dash Angostura bitters

*Stir over ice. Strain into a cocktail glass.*

## Pernod Frappé

**❚❚❚** Pernod

**❚** Anisette

**❚** fresh cream

1 egg white

*Shake over ice. Strain into small wine glasses filled with crushed ice.*

## Red Witch

**❚❚** Pernod

**❚** blackcurrant cordial

chilled sparkling cider

*Shake Pernod and cordial over ice and strain into small wine glasses. Top with cider.*

---

The ❚ symbol in the recipes is a 'unit' to indicate proportions. A reasonable single measure to use in mixing is about an ounce – equivalent to 30 millilitres (ml). Quantities in the recipes given as dashes, spoonfuls etc., are based on one-ounce unit measures of the accompanying principal ingredients. A cocktail incorporating 2 to 3 measures of alcoholic ingredients makes a reasonably strong drink for one person. Cocktails with 4 or more measures are best made for two or more people.

## Suisse

- pastis
- 4 dashes Anisette
- 1 egg white

*Shake over ice. Strain into a cocktail glass.*

## Tiger by the Tail

- pastis
- chilled orange juice

*Pour pastis into an ice-filled tall glass. Top with orange juice and add a lemon or lime slice.*

## TNT

- pastis
- rye whiskey

*Stir over ice. Strain into a cocktail glass.*

## Victory

- pastis
- grenadine
- soda water

*Stir pastis and grenadine over ice. Strain into a wine glass and top with soda.*

## Which Way

- pastis
- Anisette
- brandy

*Stir over ice. Strain into a cocktail glass.*

## Whoopee

- pastis
- apple brandy
- brandy

*Stir over ice. Strain into a cocktail glass.*

## Yellow Parrot

- pastis
- apricot brandy
- yellow Chartreuse

*Stir over ice. Strain into a cocktail glass.*

## Zammo

- pastis
- dry gin
- dash Bénédictine

*Stir over ice. Strain into a cocktail glass.*

# BRANDY

For mixing purposes, use inexpensive (or relatively inexpensive) brandy. Three-star will taste pretty much as good as XO when blended with liqueurs and fruit juices. Note that cognac and armagnac, the brandies of France, are very much drier in style than their cheaper counterparts from elsewhere in Europe or from South Africa and the United States. Where recipes here call for the sweeter style, Spanish brandy is specified.

Marc, grappa, bagaceira and other fiery grape spirits made from the rehydrated detritus of wine pressings can be substituted for the brandy in some of these recipes. If you like these rugged spirits, the resulting cocktails should be likable, too. But don't treat cocktails as camouflage for ingredients not otherwise to your taste. No amount of mixing will truly sublimate flavours (especially in spirits) that you dislike.

## American Beauty

- brandy
- dry vermouth
- grenadine
- fresh orange juice

dash crème de menthe

*Shake over ice. Strain into a cocktail glass and add a dash of port.*

## Atom Bomb

- brandy
- pastis

*Stir over ice. Strain into a cocktail glass.*

## B & B

- brandy
- Bénédictine

*Stir over ice. Strain into a cocktail glass.*

## Barney Barnato

- ♣ brandy
- ♣ Capéritif

dash Angostura bitters

dash curaçao

*Stir over ice. Strain into a cocktail glass.*

## Beagle

- ♣♣ brandy
- ♣ cranberry juice

3 dashes kümmel

dash lemon juice

*Shake over ice. Strain into a cocktail glass.*

## Betsy Ross

- ♣ brandy
- ♣ port

dash triple sec

*Stir over ice. Strain into a cocktail glass.*

## Big Boy

- ♣♣ brandy
- ♣ Cointreau
- ♣ lemon juice

*Shake over ice. Strain into a cocktail glass.*

## Block and Tackle

- ♣♣ brandy
- ♣♣ Cointreau
- ♣ apple brandy
- ♣ pastis

*Stir over ice. Strain into cocktail glasses.*

## Blue Train

- ♣♣ brandy
- ♣ pineapple syrup

chillèd sparkling wine

*Shake brandy and syrup over ice. Strain into a wine glass and top up with sparkling wine.*

---

The ♣ symbol in the recipes is a 'unit' to indicate proportions. A reasonable single measure to use in mixing is about an ounce – equivalent to 30 millilitres (ml). Quantities in the recipes given as dashes, spoonfuls etc., are based on one-ounce unit measures of the accompanying principal ingredients. A cocktail incorporating 2 to 3 measures of alcoholic ingredients makes a reasonably strong drink for one person. Cocktails with 4 or more measures are best made for two or more people.

## Bombay

- ▌▌ brandy
- ▌ dry vermouth
- ▌ sweet vermouth
- 2 dashes curaçao
- dash pastis

*Stir over ice. Strain into a cocktail glass.*

## Booster

- ▌▌ brandy
- 2 dashes curaçao
- 1 egg white

*Shake over ice. Strain into a cocktail glass and grate nutmeg over.*

## Bosom Caresser

- ▌ brandy
- ▌ madeira
- 2 dashes triple sec

*Stir over ice. Strain into a cocktail glass.*

## Brandy Alexander

- ▌ brandy
- ▌ crème de cacao
- ▌ fresh double cream

*Shake over ice. Strain into an ice-filled tall glass.*

## Brandy Blazer

- ▌▌ warmed brandy
- strip lemon peel
- strip orange peel
- sugar lump

*Put all ingredients in a sturdy tumbler. With care, set alight. Stir with a long-handled metal spoon. Strain into a cocktail glass.*

## Brandy Cassis

- ▌▌ brandy
- ▌ lemon juice
- teaspoon crème de cassis

*Shake over ice. Strain into a cocktail glass.*

---

'Claret is the liquor for boys; port, for men; but he who aspires to be a hero must drink brandy.'

Samuel Johnson, 1779

## Brandy Cocktail

❚❚❚ brandy

❚ curaçao

*Stir over ice. Strain into a cocktail glass.*

## Brandy Collins

❚❚ brandy

❚ lemon juice

teaspoon sugar

soda water

*Shake brandy, lemon and sugar over ice. Strain into a tall, ice-filled glass. Top with soda. Add an orange slice.*

## Brandy Crusta

❚❚❚ brandy

❚ curaçao

4 dashes lemon juice

3 dashes maraschino

dash Angostura bitters

lemon juice

caster sugar

*Shake over ice. Strain into a wine glass which has first been dipped in lemon juice and then caster sugar to frost the rim. Add ice cubes and a twist of lemon peel.*

## Brandy Daisy

❚❚ brandy

❚ lemon juice

teaspoon grenadine

pinch of sugar

*Shake over ice. Strain into an ice-filled tumbler. Add lemon slice and a maraschino cherry.*

## Brandy Fix

❚❚ brandy

❚ cherry brandy

❚ lemon juice

2 teaspoons sugar

*Combine in a small glass. Add crushed ice and a slice of lemon. Stir, and drink with a straw.*

## Brandy Fizz

❚❚ brandy

❚ lemon juice

teaspoon sugar

soda water

*Shake over ice. Strain into a tumbler and top with soda.*

## Brandy Flip

▮▮ brandy

1 egg

teaspoon sugar

*Shake over ice. Strain into a cocktail glass.*

## Brandy Ginger

▮▮▮ brandy

▮ ginger wine

▮ equal mix fresh lime juice and orange juice

*Shake over ice. Strain into cocktail glasses.*

## Brandy Gump

▮ brandy

▮ lemon juice

2 dashes grenadine

*Shake over ice. Strain into a cocktail glass.*

## Brandy Julep

▮▮ brandy

teaspoon sugar

4 fresh mint leaves

*Put ingredients into a tall glass and fill up with crushed ice. Gently stir with a spoon to blend. Add a lemon slice and serve with straws.*

## Brandy Moo

▮ brandy

▮▮▮ fresh milk

teaspoon sugar

*Shake over ice. Strain into a tumbler.*

## Brandy Port

▮▮ brandy

▮▮ port

▮ lemon juice

*Shake over ice. Strain into cocktail glasses.*

'Have ready a bottle of brandy, because I always feel like drinking that heroic drink when we talk ontological heroics together.'

Herman Melville in a letter to
Nathaniel Hawthorne, 1851

## Brandy Punch

3 bottles brandy

half pint (0.25 litre) Cointreau

2 pints (1 litre) chilled soda water

1 pint (0.5 litre) mixed orange and lemon juice

half pint (0.25 litre) grenadine

tablespoon sugar

*Prepare a large block of ice by freezing water in an old ice cream container. Place the block in a punch bowl and add all the ingredients, leaving the soda until last. Float fruit slices on top.*

## Brandy Sangaree

▮▮ brandy

▮ port

teaspoon sugar syrup

soda water

*Pour brandy and syrup into a tall ice-filled glass. Add soda and stir. Pour port gently on top, without stirring. Add a pinch of nutmeg (optional).*

## Brandy Sling

▮▮ brandy

▮ lemon juice

teaspoon sugar

*Stir lemon and sugar with ice in a small wine glass and add brandy.*

---

The ▮ symbol in the recipes is a 'unit' to indicate proportions. A reasonable single measure to use in mixing is about an ounce – equivalent to 30 millilitres (ml). Quantities in the recipes given as dashes, spoonfuls etc., are based on one-ounce unit measures of the accompanying principal ingredients. A cocktail incorporating 2 to 3 measures of alcoholic ingredients makes a reasonably strong drink for one person. Cocktails with 4 or more measures are best made for two or more people.

## Brandy Sour

- ▮▮ brandy
- ▮ lemon juice
- teaspoon sugar

*Shake over ice. Strain into a cocktail glass. According to personal taste, boost the sourness of this classic cocktail by reducing the proportion of sugar.*

*Sours can also be made with whisky and clear spirits.*

## Brandy Vermouth

- ▮▮▮ brandy
- ▮ sweet vermouth
- dash Angostura bitters

*Stir over ice. Strain into a cocktail glass.*

## Breakfast Egg Nogg

- ▮ brandy
- ▮▮▮ milk
- ▮ curaçao
- 1 egg

*Shake over ice. Strain into a tumbler.*

## Bull's Eye

- ▮ brandy
- ▮▮ cider
- chilled dry ginger ale

*Pour brandy and cider into a tall, ice-filled glass. Top with ginger ale.*

## Button Hook

- ▮ brandy
- ▮ apricot brandy
- ▮ crème de menthe
- ▮ pastis

*Stir over ice. Strain into cocktail glasses.*

## Capri

- ▮▮▮ brandy
- ▮ sweet vermouth
- 4 dashes Campari

*Stir over ice. Strain into cocktail glasses and add a maraschino cherry.*

## Carrol

- ▮▮ brandy
- ▮ sweet vermouth

*Stir over ice. Strain into a cocktail glass and add a pickled walnut or onion.*

## Champs-Elysées

- ▮▮▮ cognac
- ▮ Chartreuse
- ▮▮ lemon juice

teaspoon sugar

dash Angostura bitters

*Shake over ice. Strain into cocktail glasses.*

## Charles

- ▮ brandy
- ▮ sweet vermouth

dash Angostura bitters

*Stir over ice. Strain into a cocktail glass.*

## Chartreuse Daisy

- ▮▮ brandy
- ▮ green Chartreuse

4 dashes lemon juice

chilled sparkling water

*Shake spirits and juice over ice. Strain into small wine glasses and top with sparkling water.*

## Cherry Blossom

- ▮▮ brandy
- ▮▮ cherry brandy

dash curaçao

dash grenadine

dash lemon juice

*Shake over ice. Strain into cocktail glasses.*

---

'A mixture of brandy and water spoils two good things.'

Charles Lamb

## Chicago

> **▮** brandy
>
> dash curaçao
>
> dash Angostura bitters
>
> chilled sparkling wine
>
> lemon juice
>
> caster sugar

*Stir brandy, curaçao and bitters over ice. Strain into a wine glass which has first been dipped in lemon juice and then caster sugar to frost the rim. Top with sparkling wine.*

## Chief Mouse

> **▮** armagnac
>
> **▮** marc de Bourgogne
>
> chilled dry ginger ale

*Pour spirits into a tumbler filled with ice. Top with ginger ale and stir.*

## Cider Cup

> **▮▮** brandy
>
> **▮▮** Cointreau
>
> 1 pint (0.5 litre) chilled dry cider
>
> half pint (0.25 litre) chilled soda water
>
> tablespoon sugar

*Mix in a jug with ice. Add fruit slices and mint sprigs and serve in wine glasses.*

## Classic

> **▮▮▮** brandy
>
> **▮** curaçao
>
> **▮** maraschino
>
> **▮** lemon juice
>
> lemon juice
>
> caster sugar

*Shake first four ingredients over ice. Strain into a cocktail glass which has first been dipped in lemon juice and then caster sugar to frost the rim. Add a twist of lemon peel.*

## Cognac Combo

▌▌ cognac

▌ port

▌ pastis

4 dashes lemon juice

*Shake over ice. Strain into cocktail glasses.*

## Cold Deck

▌▌ brandy

▌ sweet vermouth

▌ white crème de menthe

*Stir over ice. Strain into a cocktail glass.*

## Coronation

▌▌ brandy

3 dashes curaçao

dash peppermint cordial

dash peach bitters

*Stir over ice. Strain into a cocktail glass.*

## Corpse Reviver

▌▌ brandy

▌ apple brandy

▌ sweet vermouth

*Stir over ice. Strain into a cocktail glass.*

*An evening-before, rather than a morning-after, cocktail.*

## Cuban

▌▌ brandy

▌ apricot brandy

▌ fresh lime juice

*Shake over ice. Strain into a cocktail glass.*

## Davis Brandy

▌▌ brandy

▌ dry vermouth

4 dashes grenadine

dash Angostura bitters

*Shake over ice. Strain into a cocktail glass.*

## Deauville

- ✶✶ brandy
- ✶ apple brandy
- ✶ Cointreau
- ✶ lemon juice

*Shake over ice. Strain into cocktail glasses.*

## Depth Bomb

- ✶ brandy
- ✶ apple brandy
- 4 dashes grenadine
- dash lemon juice

*Shake over ice. Strain into a cocktail glass.*

## Dolores

- ✶ Jerez (Spanish) brandy
- ✶ cherry brandy
- ✶ crème de cacao

*Stir over ice. Strain into a cocktail glass.*

## Dream

- ✶✶ brandy
- ✶ curaçao
- dash pastis

*Stir over ice. Strain into a cocktail glass.*

## East India

- ✶✶✶ brandy
- ✶ orange curaçao
- ✶ pineapple juice
- dash Angostura bitters

*Shake over ice. Strain into cocktail glasses.*

---

The ✶ symbol in the recipes is a 'unit' to indicate proportions. A reasonable single measure to use in mixing is about an ounce – equivalent to 30 millilitres (ml). Quantities in the recipes given as dashes, spoonfuls etc., are based on one-ounce unit measures of the accompanying principal ingredients. A cocktail incorporating 2 to 3 measures of alcoholic ingredients makes a reasonably strong drink for one person. Cocktails with 4 or more measures are best made for two or more people.

## Executive Suite

▮▮ brandy

▮ Grand Marnier

dash orange bitters

chilled sparkling wine

*Pour spirits and bitters into a champagne glass and top with sparkling wine.*

## Fantasia

▮▮ brandy

▮ dry vermouth

3 dashes crème de menthe

3 dashes maraschino

*Stir over ice. Strain into a cocktail glass.*

## FBR

▮▮▮ brandy

▮▮ rum

4 dashes lemon juice

1 egg white

teaspoon sugar

*Shake over ice. Strain into wine glasses half-filled with crushed ice.*

*Initials stand for Frozen Brandy and Rum.*

---

'You would have been amused by the Prime Minister last night. He did himself fairly well – not more than most gentlemen used to drink when I was a boy, but in this abstemious age it is noticeable if an extra glass or two is taken by anyone! The PM seemed to like our brandy. He had a couple of glasses (big sherry-glass size) before I left the table at 9.30, and apparently he had several more before I saw him again. By that time his legs were unsteady, but his head was quite clear, and he was able to read a map and discuss the situation with me. Indeed he was most charming and quite alert in mind.'

Field Marshal Haig on H. H. Asquith, 1916

## Fioupe

- brandy
- sweet vermouth
- teaspoon Bénédictine

*Stir over ice. Strain into a cocktail glass. Add cocktail cherry and squeeze lemon peel over.*

## Fontainebleau

- brandy
- lemon juice
- dry vermouth

*Shake over ice. Strain into cocktail glasses.*

## Four Score

- brandy
- Lillet
- yellow Chartreuse

*Stir over ice. Strain into cocktail glasses.*

## Frank Sullivan

- brandy
- Cointreau
- Lillet
- lemon juice

*Shake over ice. Strain into a cocktail glass.*

## French Connection

- brandy
- amaretto

*Stir over ice. Strain into a cocktail glass.*

## Froupe

- brandy
- sweet vermouth
- Bénédictine

*Stir over ice. Strain into a cocktail glass.*

## Gazette

- brandy
- sweet vermouth
- 3 dashes lemon juice
- teaspoon sugar

*Shake over ice. Strain into a cocktail glass.*

## Greek

■ ■ ■ Greek (Metaxa)
brandy

■ lemon juice

teaspoon ouzo

chilled dry ginger ale

*Shake over ice. Strain into
cocktail glasses.*

## Grenadier

■ ■ brandy

■ ginger wine

teaspoon sugar

*Stir over ice. Strain into a
cocktail glass.*

## Harry's Pick-Me-Up

■ ■ brandy

■ lemon juice

teaspoon grenadine

chilled champagne

*Shake the brandy, juice and
grenadine over ice. Strain into
a wine glass and top with
champagne.*

## Harvard

■ brandy

■ sweet vermouth

2 dashes Angostura bitters

dash sugar syrup

*Shake over ice. Strain into a
cocktail glass.*

## Heavenly

■ ■ ■ brandy

■ cherry brandy

■ plum brandy

*Stir over ice. Strain into
cocktail glasses.*

## Hell

■ cognac

■ crème de menthe

cayenne pepper

*Stir the spirits over ice. Strain
into a cocktail glass and add a
pinch of the cayenne.*

## Hennessy Martini

■ ■ Hennessy Cognac
VSOP

teaspoon lemon juice

*Stir gently over ice. Strain into
a cocktail glass.*

## Hoopla

- ⚍ brandy
- ⚍ Cointreau
- ⚍ Lillet
- ⚍ lemon juice

*Shake over ice. Strain into a cocktail glass.*

## IBF Pick-Me-Up

- ⚍ brandy
- 3 dashes curaçao
- 3 dashes Fernet Branca
- chilled champagne

*Mix spirits in a wine glass. Top with champagne.*

## Ichbien

- ⚍⚍ brandy
- ⚍ orange curaçao
- ⚍⚍⚍⚍ milk
- 1 egg yolk

*Shake over ice. Strain into cocktail glasses and sprinkle a pinch of ground nutmeg over.*

## Iolanthe

- ⚍⚍ brandy
- ⚍ Lillet
- ⚍ Grand Marnier
- ⚍ orange juice
- dash orange bitters

*Shake over ice. Strain into cocktail glasses.*

---

The ⚍ symbol in the recipes is a 'unit' to indicate proportions. A reasonable single measure to use in mixing is about an ounce – equivalent to 30 millilitres (ml). Quantities in the recipes given as dashes, spoonfuls etc., are based on one-ounce unit measures of the accompanying principal ingredients. A cocktail incorporating 2 to 3 measures of alcoholic ingredients makes a reasonably strong drink for one person. Cocktails with 4 or more measures are best made for two or more people.

## Japanese

- **❚** brandy
- 4 dashes fresh lime juice
- 3 dashes orgeat syrup
- dash Angostura bitters

*Shake over ice. Strain into a cocktail glass.*

## Jersey Lightning

- **❚❚** brandy
- **❚** apple brandy
- **❚** sweet vermouth
- dash Angostura bitters

*Stir over ice. Strain into cocktail glasses.*

## Lady Be Good

- **❚❚** brandy
- **❚** crème de menthe
- **❚** sweet vermouth

*Stir over ice. Strain into cocktail glasses.*

## La Jolla

- **❚❚❚** brandy
- **❚** banana liqueur
- **❚** mixed lemon and orange juice

*Shake over ice. Strain into cocktail glasses.*

*Named after the resort suburb of San Diego, California, and locally pronounced La Hoya.*

## Lilliput

- **❚** brandy
- **❚** Lillet
- **❚** lemon juice
- dash white curaçao

*Shake over ice. Strain into a cocktail glass.*

## Lugger

- **❚** brandy
- **❚** apple brandy
- dash apricot brandy

*Stir over ice. Strain into a cocktail glass.*

## Metropolitan

- brandy
- sweet vermouth

dash Angostura bitters

sprinkling sugar

*Shake over ice. Strain into a cocktail glass.*

## Mikado

- brandy

teaspoon crème de cacao

2 dashes crème de noyaux

dash Angostura bitters

*Stir over ice. Strain into a cocktail glass.*

## Montana

- brandy
- port
- dry vermouth

2 dashes Angostura bitters

*Stir over ice. Strain into cocktail glasses.*

## Moonraker

- brandy
- peach brandy
- quinquina

dash pastis

*Stir over ice. Strain into a cocktail glass.*

## Morning

- brandy
- dry vermouth

2 dashes curaçao

2 dashes maraschino

2 dashes orange bitters

2 dashes pastis

*Stir over ice. Strain into a cocktail glass.*

## Netherland

- brandy
- triple sec

dash orange bitters

*Stir over ice. Strain into a cocktail glass.*

## Newton's Special

- ✷✷✷ brandy
- ✷ Cointreau
- dash Angostura bitters

*Stir over ice. Strain into a cocktail glass.*

## Nick's Own

- ✷ brandy
- ✷ sweet vermouth
- dash Angostura bitters
- dash pastis

*Stir over ice. Strain into a cocktail glass, add maraschino cherry and squeeze lemon peel over.*

## Night Cap

- ✷ brandy
- 1 egg, beaten lightly
- tablespoon honey
- warmed milk

*Warm a mug and add the brandy, egg and honey. Top with milk and stir.*

## Odd McIntyre

- ✷ brandy
- ✷ Lillet
- ✷ Cointreau
- ✷ lemon juice

*Shake over ice. Strain into cocktail glasses.*

## Olympic

- ✷ brandy
- ✷ curaçao
- ✷ orange juice

*Shake over ice. Strain into a cocktail glass.*

## Philadelphia

- ✷✷ brandy
- ✷ curaçao
- dash pastis

*Stir over ice. Strain into a cocktail glass.*

## Phoebe Snow

- ✷ brandy
- ✷ Dubonnet
- dash pastis

*Stir over ice. Strain into a cocktail glass.*

## Pisco Sour

- ▌▌ pisco
- ▌ lemon juice
- teaspoon sugar
- dash Angostura bitters

*Shake over ice. Strain into a cocktail glass.*

*Pisco is the colourless grape brandy of Chile (and Peru).*

## Pisco Special

- ▌▌ pisco
- ▌ lemon juice
- teaspoon sugar
- 1 egg white
- dash Angostura bitters

*Prepare a small brandy glass by dipping the rim in lemon juice and then sugar to encrust. Shake all ingredients over ice and strain.*

## Polonaise

- ▌▌▌ brandy
- ▌ blackberry liqueur
- ▌ dry sherry
- 4 dashes lemon juice

*Shake over ice. Strain into cocktail glasses.*

## Poop Deck

- ▌ brandy
- ▌ port
- teaspoon blackberry liqueur

*Stir over ice. Strain into a cocktail glass.*

'Napoleon' brandy is a quality grade for cognac, signifying the spirit has had at least five years' ageing. Bottles of the original Napoleon brandy, produced for Napoléon Bonaparte and branded with the imperial 'N' in 1811, are said still to exist, but are unlikely to make pleasant drinking today.

## Prairie Oyster

> ▌ brandy

> ▌ equal mix of wine vinegar and Worcestershire sauce

> dollop tomato ketchup

> pinch cayenne pepper

> 1 egg yolk

*Shake all but the egg and cayenne over ice. Strain into a small tumbler and add the egg yolk, taking care to keep it intact. Sprinkle cayenne over.*

*Allegedly a sovereign remedy for hangovers. The drink is supposed to be swallowed in one brave gulp.*

## Presto

> ▌ brandy

> 4 dashes sweet vermouth

> 4 dashes orange juice

> dash pastis

*Shake over ice. Strain into a cocktail glass.*

## Quaker's

> ▌▌ brandy

> ▌▌ rum

> ▌ lemon juice

> ▌ raspberry syrup

*Shake over ice. Strain into cocktail glasses.*

## Quelle Vie

> ▌▌ brandy

> ▌ kümmel

*Stir over ice. Strain into a cocktail glass.*

---

The ▌ symbol in the recipes is a 'unit' to indicate proportions. A reasonable single measure to use in mixing is about an ounce – equivalent to 30 millilitres (ml). Quantities in the recipes given as dashes, spoonfuls etc., are based on one-ounce unit measures of the accompanying principal ingredients. A cocktail incorporating 2 to 3 measures of alcoholic ingredients makes a reasonably strong drink for one person. Cocktails with 4 or more measures are best made for two or more people.

## Ray Long

∎∎ brandy

∎ sweet vermouth

4 dashes pastis

dash Angostura bitters

*Stir over ice. Strain into a cocktail glass.*

## Rolls Royce

∎∎ cognac

∎ Cointreau

∎∎ orange juice

*Shake over ice. Strain into cocktail glasses.*

*Another Rolls Royce recipe, entirely different from this American version, appears in the Gin section.*

## Rue de la Paix

∎ brandy

∎ dry vermouth

4 dashes curaçao

4 dashes maraschino

4 dashes pastis

2 dashes orange bitters

*Stir over ice. Strain into a cocktail glass.*

## Sangaree

∎∎ brandy

∎ sugared water

teaspoon port

chilled soda water

pinch nutmeg

*Pour brandy and sugared water over ice in a tumbler. Top with soda, stir and float port on top. Sprinkle nutmeg over.*

*Sangarees can be made with any spirit base.*

## Saratoga

∎ brandy

2 dashes Angostura bitters

2 dashes maraschino

small slice pineapple

soda water

*Shake brandy, bitters, maraschino and fruit over ice. Strain into a brandy glass and add a splash of soda.*

## Savoy Corpse Reviver

- ⚊ brandy
- ⚊ Fernet Branca
- ⚊ white crème de menthe

*Stir over ice. Strain into a cocktail glass.*

## Sidecar

- ⚊⚊ brandy
- ⚊ Cointreau
- ⚊ lemon juice

*Shake over ice. Strain into a cocktail glass.*

## Sir Walter

- ⚊ brandy
- ⚊ rum
- 4 dashes curaçao
- 4 dashes grenadine
- 4 dashes lemon juice

*Shake over ice. Strain into a cocktail glass.*

Sir Walter Raleigh, a notorious womaniser, was nevertheless sensitive about his reputation. In his masterpiece of gossip, *Brief Lives*, John Aubrey tells the story of Sir Walter's dissolute son, who embarrassed the great man at an important banquet.

'He sat next to his father and was very demure at least half dinner time. Then, said he, "I, this morning, not having the fear of God before my eyes but by the instigation of the devil, went to a whore. I was very eager of her, kissed and embraced her, and went to enjoy her, but she thrust me from her, and vowed I should not, 'for your father lay with me but an hour ago'."

'Sir Walt, being so strangely surprised and put out of his countenance at so great a table, gives his son a damned blow over the face. His son, as rude as he was, would not strike his father, but strikes over the face the gentleman that sat next to him and said, "Box about: 'twill come to my father anon".'

## Sleepy Head

- brandy
- strip orange peel
- sprig mint
- dry ginger ale

*Put brandy, peel and mint in a tumbler with ice. Top with ginger ale.*

## Stinger

- brandy
- white crème de menthe

*Stir over ice. Strain into cocktail glasses.*

## Stirrup Cup

- brandy
- cherry brandy
- lemon juice
- teaspoon sugar

*Shake over ice. Strain into an ice-filled tumbler.*

## Stomach Reviver

- brandy
- Fernet Branca
- 4 dashes Angostura bitters

*Stir over ice. Strain into a cocktail glass.*

## Third Rail

- brandy
- apple brandy
- rum
- dash pastis

*Stir over ice. Strain into a cocktail glass.*

## Three Miller

- brandy
- rum
- 4 dashes grenadine
- dash lemon juice

*Shake over ice. Strain into a cocktail glass.*

## Thunder

- brandy
- 1 egg yolk
- teaspoon sugar
- dash Tabasco

*Shake over ice. Strain into a cocktail glass.*

## Vanderbilt

- ▮ ▮ ▮ brandy
- ▮ cherry brandy
- 2 dashes sugar syrup
- dash Angostura bitters

*Shake over ice. Strain into cocktail glasses.*

## Via Veneto

- ▮ ▮ ▮ brandy
- ▮ Sambuca
- ▮ lemon juice
- teaspoon sugar
- 1 egg white

*Shake over ice. Strain into cocktail glasses.*

## Waterbury

- ▮ ▮ brandy
- ▮ lemon juice
- 1 egg white
- sprinkle of sugar

*Shake over ice. Strain into a cocktail glass.*

## Welcome Stranger

- ▮ brandy
- ▮ gin
- ▮ Swedish Punsch
- ▮ grenadine
- ▮ lemon juice
- ▮ orange juice

*Shake over ice. Strain into cocktail glasses.*

## Whip

- ▮ ▮ brandy
- ▮ dry vermouth
- ▮ sweet vermouth
- 3 dashes curaçao
- dash pastis

*Shake over ice. Strain into cocktail glasses.*

## Willie Smith

- ▮ ▮ brandy
- ▮ maraschino
- dash lemon juice

*Shake over ice. Strain into a cocktail glass.*

# CHAMPAGNE *and sparkling wine*

Good champagne is expensive, and bad champagne only marginally less so. Unless the real thing – that is, *le* champagne from *La* Champagne in France, is specified, it is a rational economy to opt for some other dry (or *brut*) sparkler. From elsewhere in France, sparkling Saumur and Blanquette de Limoux offer good value. Cava from Spain is inexpensive and of almost uniformly high quality, and the dry sparkling wines of California, Australia and New Zealand can be excellent.

## Bellini

chilled champagne

❚ fresh peach juice

dash grenadine

*Fill a good-sized wine glass with ice (preferably crushed) and pour over the peach juice, then the grenadine. Top with champagne. Add a slice of fresh peach.*

*Famed recipe of Harry's Bar, Venice, named after Giovanni Bellini (1430–1516), a leading artist of the Venetian school of painting at the time of the Renaissance.*

## Black Velvet

❚ chilled champagne

❚ chilled stout

*Gently pour into a champagne glass. Do not stir.*

*Said to have been devised by Prince Otto von Bismarck, first Chancellor of Germany (1815–98).*

## Bolly-Stolly

**❚❚❚❚** chilled Bollinger NV champagne

**❚** chilled Stolichnaya vodka

*Pour into a champagne glass.*

*Mythical but memorable device of Jennifer Saunders for BBC television comedy drama* Absolutely Fabulous.

## Bucks Fizz

chilled sparkling wine

chilled fresh orange juice

*Into a champagne flûte or wine glass, pour the sparkling wine first, then add an equal quantity of orange.*

*Devised at Buck's club, London, and originally made with Bollinger Champagne.*

## Champagne Cocktail

teaspoon brandy

2 dashes Angostura bitters

sugar lump

chilled champagne or sparkling wine

*Soak sugar lump with the bitters and place in a champagne glass. Add brandy. Top up with champagne.*

## Champagne Cobbler

**❚** brandy

**❚** curaçao

chilled champagne

*Pour spirits over ice in a large wine glass. Top with champagne. Add an orange slice.*

---

The ❚ symbol in the recipes is a 'unit' to indicate proportions. A reasonable single measure to use in mixing is about an ounce – equivalent to 30 millilitres (ml). Quantities in the recipes given as dashes, spoonfuls etc., are based on one-ounce unit measures of the accompanying principal ingredients. A cocktail incorporating 2 to 3 measures of alcoholic ingredients makes a reasonably strong drink for one person. Cocktails with 4 or more measures are best made for two or more people.

## Champagne Cooler

- ⚡ brandy
- ⚡ Cointreau
- chilled champagne

*Pour spirits over ice in a large wine glass. Top with champagne. Add a mint sprig.*

## Champagne Cup

- ⚡⚡⚡⚡ brandy
- ⚡⚡⚡ maraschino
- ⚡⚡ Bénédictine
- bottle of champagne, chilled
- 2 pints (1 litre) sparkling water, chilled
- orange and lemon slices

*Place sliced fruit in a large jug and add spirits. Leave for half and hour. Add a handful of ice cubes and pour in the champagne and sparkling water immediately before serving in wine glasses.*

*An excellent way of improving the enjoyment of inferior champagne.*

## Champagne Normandy

- ⚡ calvados
- teaspoon sugar
- dash Angostura bitters
- chilled champagne

*In a champagne glass, dissolve the sugar in the calvados and add bitters. Top with champagne. Add an orange slice.*

## Champagne Pick-Me-Up

- ⚡⚡ brandy
- ⚡⚡ lemon and orange juice
- 4 dashes grenadine
- chilled champagne

*Shake brandy, fruit juice and grenadine over ice. Strain into wine glasses and top with champagne.*

---

I wish I had drunk more champagne.

> J. Maynard Keynes admitting
> to the principal among his regrets.

## Champagne Sidecar

**ı ı** brandy

**ı** Cointreau

**ı** lemon juice

chilled champagne or sparkling wine

*Shake first three ingredients over ice. Strain into a champagne glass and top up with champagne.*

## Dawn

**ı** chilled champagne

**ı** chilled fino sherry

**ı** chilled fresh lime juice

*Stir and serve in a cocktail glass.*

> George 'Beau' Brummell (1788–1840), the Regency dandy who spent the first five hours of each day getting washed and dressed, insisted on having his boots polished with champagne.

## Diamond Fizz

**ı ı** dry gin

**ı** lemon juice

teaspoon caster sugar

chilled sparkling wine

*Shake gin, lemon and sugar and strain into a tall, ice-filled glass. Top with sparkling wine and stir.*

## Ducks Fizz

chilled Canard-Duchêne champagne

chilled fresh orange juice

*Into a champagne flûte or wine glass, pour the champagne first, then add an equal quantity of orange.*

## Kir Royale

teaspoon crème de cassis

chilled champagne

*Place cassis in a champagne glass. Fill up with champagne. This drink is also an improver of ordinary sparkling wines.*

## Mimosa

chilled sparkling wine

chilled orange juice

*Pour equal measures over ice in a large wine glass and stir.*

## Rikki-Tikki-Tavi

teaspoon brandy

teaspoon curaçao

Angostura bitters

sugar lump

chilled champagne

*Drop the sugar lump into a champagne flûte and infuse with the bitters. The lump should turn red, but not disintegrate. Add the brandy and curaçao. Top with champagne.*

## Sitges

⚡ Spanish brandy

⚡ orange juice

dash orange bitters

chilled cava (Spanish sparkling wine)

*Shake all but the cava over ice and strain into a wine glass. Top with cava and stir.*

We sit at our tables and tipple champagne;
Ere one bottle goes, comes another again;
The waiters they skip and they scuttle about,
And the landlord attends us so civilly out.
So pleasant it is to have money, heigh ho!
So pleasant it is to have money.

Arthur Hugh Clough, *Dipsychus*

# FRUIT BRANDIES

Apple (or cider) brandy is known as applejack in the US and as calvados in France. These brandies are the principal ingredients in many classic cocktails, and a subsidiary ingredient in countless others. Cocktail enthusiasts should regard apple brandy as a necessity. Other fruit brandies that feature in numerous recipes are apricot and cherry. Peach occurs rather less frequently.

## Adam's Apple

- ❚❚ calvados
- ❚ dry gin
- ❚ dry vermouth
- 2 dashes yellow Chartreuse

*Stir over ice. Strain into a cocktail glass.*

## After Dinner

- ❚ apricot brandy
- ❚ Cointreau
- ❚ fresh lime juice

*Shake over ice. Strain into a cocktail glass.*

## After Dinner 2

- ❚ cherry brandy
- ❚ prunelle liqueur
- ❚ lemon juice

*Shake over ice. Strain into a cocktail glass.*

## After Supper

- ❚ apricot brandy
- ❚ Cointreau
- ❚ lemon juice

*Shake over ice. Strain into a cocktail glass.*

# Apple

- ✴ ✴ apple brandy
- ✴ ✴ sweet cider
- ✴ gin
- ✴ brandy

*Shake over ice. Strain into cocktail glasses.*

# Apple Blow Fizz

- ✴ apple brandy

  teaspoon lemon juice

  teaspoon powdered sugar

  1 egg white

*Shake over ice. Strain into a medium-sized stemmed glass and top with soda.*

# Applejack

- ✴ apple brandy
- ✴ sweet vermouth

  dash Angostura bitters

*Shake over ice. Strain into a cocktail glass.*

# Applejack Rabbit

- ✴ apple brandy
- ✴ lemon juice
- ✴ orange juice
- ✴ maple syrup

*Shake over ice. Strain into a cocktail glass.*

---

The ✴ symbol in the recipes is a 'unit' to indicate proportions. A reasonable single measure to use in mixing is about an ounce – equivalent to 30 millilitres (ml). Quantities in the recipes given as dashes, spoonfuls etc., are based on one-ounce unit measures of the accompanying principal ingredients. A cocktail incorporating 2 to 3 measures of alcoholic ingredients makes a reasonably strong drink for one person. Cocktails with 4 or more measures are best made for two or more people.

## Applejack Special

❚ apple brandy

❚❚ white rum

❚❚ sweet vermouth

❚ lemon juice

dash grenadine

*Shake over ice. Strain into cocktail glasses.*

## Apricot

❚❚ apricot brandy

❚ lemon juice

❚ orange juice

dash dry gin

*Shake over ice. Strain into a cocktail glass.*

## Apricot Cooler

❚ apricot brandy

❚ fresh lime juice

2 dashes grenadine

*Shake over ice. Strain into a tall glass and top with soda water.*

## Bentley

❚ apple brandy

❚ Dubonnet

*Stir over ice. Strain into a cocktail glass.*

## Bulldog

❚❚❚ cherry brandy

❚ rum

❚ fresh lime juice

*Shake over ice. Strain into cocktail glasses.*

## Calvados Cocktail

❚❚ calvados

❚ Cointreau

❚❚ orange juice

dash orange bitters

*Shake over ice. Strain into cocktail glasses.*

## Castle Dip

❚ apple brandy

❚ white crème de menthe

3 dashes pastis

*Stir over ice. Strain into a cocktail glass.*

## Cherry Blossom

- ⧗⧗ cherry brandy
- ⧗ brandy
- 4 dashes curaçao
- 4 dashes grenadine
- 4 dashes lemon juice

*Shake over ice. Strain into a cocktail glass.*

## Darb

- ⧗ apricot brandy
- ⧗ dry gin
- ⧗ dry vermouth
- 3 dashes lemon juice

*Shake over ice. Strain into a cocktail glass.*

## Deauville

- ⧗ apple brandy
- ⧗ brandy
- ⧗ Cointreau
- ⧗ lemon juice

*Shake over ice. Strain into a cocktail glass.*

## Dempsey

- ⧗ apple brandy
- ⧗ gin
- dash pastis
- dash grenadine

*Shake over ice. Strain into a cocktail glass.*

## Depth Bomb

- ⧗ apple brandy
- ⧗ brandy
- 4 dashes grenadine
- dash lemon juice

*Shake over ice. Strain into a cocktail glass.*

Calvados, the apple brandy of France, is so called after a Normandy *département* – which took the name from that of the *Calvador*, a ship of the Spanish Armada which foundered off the Normandy coast in 1588.

## Devonshire Pride

- ▮ apple brandy
- ▮ Swedish Punsch

dash lemon juice

*Shake over ice. Strain into a cocktail glass.*

## Diki-Diki

- ▮ apple brandy

4 dashes Swedish Punsch

4 dashes grapefruit juice

*Shake over ice. Strain into a cocktail glass.*

## Ethel

- ▮ apricot brandy
- ▮ curaçao
- ▮ white crème de menthe

*Stir over ice. Strain into a cocktail glass.*

## Eve O

- ▮▮ apple brandy
- ▮▮ dry gin
- ▮ fresh orange juice

dash Angostura bitters

*Stir over ice. Strain into cocktail glasses.*

## Eve's Apple

- ▮ apple brandy
- ▮ Swedish Punsch
- ▮ grapefruit juice

*Shake over ice. Strain into a cocktail glass.*

## Fairbanks

- ▮ apricot brandy
- ▮ dry gin
- ▮ dry vermouth

dash grenadine

dash lemon juice

*Shake over ice. Strain into a cocktail glass.*

---

*Eaux-de-vie* are dry, colourless spirits distilled from the fermented juice of various fruits. Fruit 'brandies' such as apricot and cherry are liqueurs based in neutral spirit and flavoured with the appropriate fruit.

## Favourite

- ✶ apricot brandy
- ✶ dry gin
- ✶ dry vermouth
- dash lemon juice

*Shake over ice. Strain into a cocktail glass.*

## Fifth Avenue

- ✶ apricot brandy
- ✶ crème de cacao
- ✶ sweetened fresh cream

*Into a small wine glass, pour each ingredient in turn. Take care to prevent them mixing.*

## Frozen Apple

- ✶✶✶ apple brandy
- ✶ fresh lime juice
- 1 egg white
- teaspoon sugar

*Shake over ice. Strain into small wine glasses half-filled with crushed ice.*

## Fruit Bat

- ✶ cider brandy
- ✶ dry vermouth
- ✶ dry sherry

*Stir over ice. Strain into a cocktail glass.*

## Gilroy

- ✶✶ cherry brandy
- ✶✶ dry gin
- ✶ dry vermouth
- ✶ lemon juice
- dash orange bitters

*Shake over ice. Strain into cocktail glasses.*

## Golden Dawn

- ✶ apple brandy
- ✶ apricot brandy
- ✶ dry gin
- ✶ orange juice
- dash grenadine

*Shake first four ingredients over ice. Strain into a cocktail glass containing the grenadine.*

# Havana

- ▮▮ apricot brandy
- ▮ dry gin
- ▮ Swedish Punsch

dash lemon juice

*Shake over ice. Strain into cocktail glasses.*

# Honeymoon

- ▮▮ apple brandy
- ▮▮ Bénédictine
- ▮ lemon juice

3 dashes curaçao

*Shake over ice. Strain into cocktail glasses.*

# Hop Toad

- ▮▮▮ apricot brandy
- ▮ lemon juice

*Shake over ice. Strain into a cocktail glass.*

# Jack in the Box

- ▮ apple brandy
- ▮ pineapple juice

dash Angostura bitters

*Shake over ice. Strain into cocktail glasses.*

# Jack Rose

- ▮▮ apple brandy
- ▮ grenadine
- ▮ lemon juice

*Shake over ice. Strain into a cocktail glass.*

# Kiss Kiss

- ▮ cherry brandy
- ▮ dry gin
- ▮ sweet vermouth

*Stir over ice. Strain into a cocktail glass.*

---

The ▮ symbol in the recipes is a 'unit' to indicate proportions. A reasonable single measure to use in mixing is about an ounce – equivalent to 30 millilitres (ml). Quantities in the recipes given as dashes, spoonfuls etc., are based on one-ounce unit measures of the accompanying principal ingredients. A cocktail incorporating 2 to 3 measures of alcoholic ingredients makes a reasonably strong drink for one person. Cocktails with 4 or more measures are best made for two or more people.

## Liberty

ı ı apple brandy

ı rum

dash sugar syrup

*Shake over ice. Strain into a
cocktail glass.*

## Margaret Rose

ı ı calvados

ı ı gin

ı Cointreau

ı lemon juice

dash grenadine

*Shake over ice. Strain into
cocktail glasses.*

## Merry Widow

ı cherry brandy

ı maraschino

*Stir over ice. Strain into a
cocktail glass.*

*Other Merry Widow recipes
appear in the Gin and Sherry
sections.*

## Millionaire

ı apricot brandy

ı rum

ı sloe gin

ı fresh lime juice

dash grenadine

*Shake over ice. Strain into
cocktail glasses.*

## Moonlight Cooler

ı ı apple brandy

ı lemon juice

teaspoon sugar

soda water

*Shake brandy, lemon and
sugar over ice. Strain into a
tall glass. Top with soda and
add fruit slices.*

## Moulin Rouge

ı ı apricot brandy

ı orange gin

ı lemon juice

3 dashes grenadine

*Shake over ice. Strain into a
cocktail glass.*

## Mule's Hind Leg

- ▮ apple brandy
- ▮ apricot brandy
- ▮ Bénédictine
- ▮ gin
- ▮ maple syrup

*Shake over ice. Strain into cocktail glasses.*

## Oom Paul

- ▮ apple brandy
- ▮ Capéritif

*Stir over ice. Strain into a cocktail glass.*

## Philadelphia Scotchman

- ▮ apple brandy
- ▮ port
- ▮ orange juice
- dry ginger ale

*Pour brandy, port and orange into a tumbler with ice. Stir and top with ginger ale.*

## Pink Whiskers

- ▮▮ apricot brandy
- ▮▮ orange juice
- ▮ dry vermouth
- 2 dashes grenadine

*Shake over ice. Strain into cocktail glasses.*

---

The Somerset Cider Brandy Co. was challenged in the European Court in 1995 over its use of the term 'brandy' for its famously delicious three- and five-year-old spirits, distilled from Somerset cider. The plaintiffs, Spain's brandy-producers, maintained that spirits must be distilled from grapes to qualify as 'brandy' – but lost the case when it was pointed out that there were precedents for 'fruit brandies'. Coincidentally, the most famous producer of cherry brandy, de Kuyper, celebrated its 200th anniversary in 1995.

## Princess

* apricot brandy

teaspoon sweetened cream

*Pour brandy into a liqueur glass. Float cream on top.*

## Puerto Apple

** apple brandy

* rum

4 dashes fresh lime juice

teaspoon sugar

*Shake over ice. Strain into a cocktail glass.*

## Rainbow's End

** apricot brandy

* cherry brandy

* banana liqueur

tablespoon fresh cream

*Shake over ice. Strain into cocktail glasses.*

## Royal

* cherry brandy

* gin

* dry vermouth

dash maraschino

*Stir over ice. Strain into a cocktail glass and add a cocktail cherry.*

## Royal Smile

** apple brandy

* dry gin

* grenadine

*Shake over ice. Strain into a cocktail glass.*

## Royal Wedding

* peach brandy

* kirsch

** orange juice

chilled sparkling wine

*Shake brandy, kirsch and orange over ice. Strain into a champagne glass and top with sparkling wine.*

## Saucy Sue

- apple brandy
- brandy

dash apricot brandy

dash pastis

*Stir over ice. Strain into a cocktail glass.*

## Savoy Tango

- apple brandy
- sloe gin

*Stir over ice. Strain into a cocktail glass.*

## Sea Breeze Cooler

- apricot brandy
- dry gin
- lemon juice

2 dashes grenadine

soda water

mint sprigs

*Shake brandy, gin, lemon and grenadine over ice. Strain into tall glasses filled with ice and top with soda. Add mint sprigs.*

## Sharky Punch

- apple brandy
- rye whiskey

chilled soda water

*Shake brandy and whiskey over ice. Strain into a tumbler and top with soda.*

## Singapore Sling

- cherry brandy
- dry gin

4 dashes lemon juice

chilled soda water

*Shake over ice. Strain into an ice-filled tumbler and top with soda.*

*Another version of this cocktail is included in the Gin section.*

## Sonora

- apple brandy
- rum

2 dashes apricot brandy

dash lemon juice

*Shake over ice. Strain into a cocktail glass.*

## Sonza's Wilson

- cherry brandy
- gin
- grenadine
- lemon juice

*Shake over ice. Strain into cocktail glasses.*

## Special Rough

- apple brandy
- brandy
- dash pastis

*Stir over ice. Strain into a cocktail glass.*

## Star

- apple brandy
- dry gin
- 4 dashes grapefruit juice
- dash dry vermouth
- dash sweet vermouth

*Shake over ice. Strain into a cocktail glass.*

## Sunburst

- apple brandy
- Grand Marnier
- dash orange bitters
- chilled sparkling wine

*Shake spirits and bitters over ice. Strain into small wine glasses and top with sparkling wine.*

## Sutton Place

- apricot brandy
- Cointreau
- crème de menthe

*Stir over ice. Strain into a cocktail glass.*

## Tempter

- apricot brandy
- port

*Stir over ice. Strain into a cocktail glass.*

## Third Rail

- apple brandy
- brandy
- rum

dash pastis

*Stir over ice. Strain into a cocktail glass.*

## Tinton

- apple brandy
- port

*Stir over ice. Strain into a cocktail glass.*

## Toby Special

- apricot brandy
- Bacardi rum
- grenadine
- lemon juice

*Shake over ice. Strain into cocktail glasses.*

## Torpedo

- apple brandy
- brandy

dash gin

*Stir over ice. Strain into a cocktail glass.*

## Tulip

- apple brandy
- sweet vermouth
- apricot brandy
- lemon juice

*Shake over ice. Strain into cocktail glasses.*

## Twelve Miles Out

- apple brandy
- rum
- Swedish Punsch

*Shake over ice. Strain into a cocktail glass and squeeze lemon peel over.*

---

'He could . . . drink more rum-toddy, mint-julep, gin-sling and cock-tail, than any private gentleman of his acquaintance.'
Charles Dickens on Major Pawkins of Pennsylvania in *Martin Chuzzlewit* (1844). Possibly the first reference to a cocktail in English literature.

## Valencia

- **‖** apricot brandy
- **‖** orange juice
- 2 dashes orange bitters

*Shake over ice. Strain into a cocktail glass.*

## Virgin's Kiss

- **‖‖‖** peach brandy
- **‖** amaretto
- **‖** fresh cream
- 2 dashes orange bitters

*Shake over ice. Strain into cocktail glasses.*

## Wallaby

- **‖** peach brandy
- **‖** Dubonnet
- 4 dashes lime juice
- dash grenadine

*Shake over ice. Strain into a cocktail glass.*

## Warday's

- **‖** apple brandy
- **‖** dry gin
- **‖** sweet vermouth
- 2 dashes Chartreuse

*Stir over ice. Strain into a cocktail glass.*

## Whist

- **‖‖** apple brandy
- **‖** rum
- **‖** sweet vermouth

*Stir over ice. Strain into a cocktail glass.*

## Whoopee

- **‖** apple brandy
- **‖** brandy
- **‖** pastis

*Stir over ice. Strain into a cocktail glass.*

## Widow's Kiss

- ⚫⚫ apple brandy
- ⚫ Bénédictine
- ⚫ Chartreuse

*Stir over ice. Strain into a cocktail glass.*

## Woodstock

- ⚫⚫ apple brandy
- ⚫ dry vermouth

*Stir over ice. Strain into a cocktail glass.*

## Yellow Parrot

- ⚫ apricot brandy
- ⚫ pastis
- ⚫ yellow Chartreuse

*Stir over ice. Strain into a cocktail glass.*

---

Glasses are raised to cordial salutations in just about every country.

Here are just a few ways of saying 'Cheers':

*All Tua Salute* – Italy

*Egészégedre* – Hungary

*Gam bay* – China

*Kampai* – Japan

*Nardorovia* – Russia

*Okole Maluna Hauoli Maoli Oe* – Hawaii

*Oogy Wawa* – Zululand

*Proost* – Netherlands

*Prosit* – Germany

*Salud* – Spain

*Schlante* – Scotland

*Sköl* – Norway and Sweden

*Slainte* – Ireland

*Steeneeyasas* – Greece

*Yum sing* – Hong Kong

*Zivio* – Serbo-Croat

# GIN

Gordon's slogan 'The heart of a good cocktail' is entirely legitimate, for gin is indeed the core ingredient of more recipes than any other spirit. In this section, nearly all the recipes are based on 'dry' gin, also known as 'London' gin after the new style of spirit distilled in the city from the seventeenth century. It became distinct from the sweeter, fuller flavours of the original gin of the Netherlands, genever. Plymouth gin is also an excellent base for all the dry gin recipes here.

Note that recipes based on sloe gin are listed in the Liqueurs and Apéritifs section.

## Abbey

- ❚❚❚ dry gin
- ❚ Lillet
- ❚❚ fresh orange juice
- dash Angostura bitters

*Stir over ice and strain into cocktail glasses. Add a maraschino cherry.*

## Abbey Bells

- ❚❚ dry gin
- ❚ apricot brandy
- ❚ fresh orange juice
- ❚ dry vermouth
- dash grenadine

*Shake over ice and strain into a cocktail glass.*

---

Work is the curse of the drinking classes.        Oscar Wilde

## Adam and Eve

■ ■ Plymouth gin

■ ■ ■ orange curaçao

■ yellow Chartreuse

*Stir over ice. Strain into a cocktail glass.*

## After One

■ dry gin

■ Campari

■ sweet vermouth

■ Galliano

*Stir over ice. Strain into a cocktail glass.*

## Alabama Fizz

■ ■ ■ dry gin

■ ■ lemon juice

teaspoon powdered sugar

*Shake over ice. Strain into tumbler and top up with soda. Add mint sprig.*

## Alaska

■ ■ ■ dry gin

■ yellow Chartreuse

*Stir over ice. Strain into a cocktail glass.*

## Albemarle Fizz

■ ■ dry gin

■ lemon juice

teaspoon powdered sugar

dash raspberry syrup

*Shake first three ingredients over ice. Strain into an ice-filled stemmed glass, top with soda and add a dash of raspberry syrup.*

## Alcudla

■ ■ dry gin

■ Galliano

■ banana liqueur

■ grapefruit juice

*Shake over ice. Strain into a cocktail glass.*

# Alexander

- ▮▮ dry gin
- ▮ crème de cacao
- ▮ fresh single cream

*Shake over ice. Strain into a cocktail glass.*

# Alexander's Sister

- ▮▮ dry gin
- ▮ crème de menthe
- ▮ fresh single cream

*Shake over ice. Strain into a cocktail glass.*

# Alexandra's Sister-in-Law

- ▮ dry gin
- ▮ crème de menthe
- ▮ fresh single cream

*Shake over ice. Strain into a cocktail glass.*

# Allen

- ▮▮ dry gin
- ▮ maraschino
- dash lemon juice

*Shake over ice. Strain into a cocktail glass.*

# Almond

- ▮▮ warmed dry gin in which a few blanched almonds have steeped until mixture has cooled
- ▮▮ sweet white wine
- ▮ dry vermouth
- 2 dashes peach brandy
- 2 dashes kirsch

*Shake over ice. Strain into a cocktail glass.*

# Angler

- ▮ dry gin
- 2 dashes orange bitters
- dash Angostura bitters
- dash grenadine

*Shake over ice. Strain into a cocktail glass.*

# Apparent

- ▮ dry gin
- ▮ Dubonnet
- dash pastis

*Stir over ice. Strain into a cocktail glass.*

## Appetizer

- ▮ dry gin
- ▮ Dubonnet
- ▮ ▮ fresh orange juice

*Shake over ice. Strain into a cocktail glass.*

## Ashes

- ▮ ▮ dry gin
- ▮ Marnique liqueur
- ▮ lemon juice
- 2 dashes yellow Chartreuse

*Shake over ice. Strain into a cocktail glass and add a maraschino cherry.*

## Astoria

- ▮ ▮ dry gin
- ▮ dry vermouth
- dash orange bitters

*Stir over ice. Strain into a cocktail glass and add a cocktail olive.*

## Atta Boy

- ▮ ▮ dry gin
- ▮ dry vermouth
- 2 dashes grenadine

*Shake over ice. Strain into a cocktail glass.*

---

The ▮ symbol in the recipes is a 'unit' to indicate proportions. A reasonable single measure to use in mixing is about an ounce – equivalent to 30 millilitres (ml). Quantities in the recipes given as dashes, spoonfuls etc., are based on one-ounce unit measures of the accompanying principal ingredients. A cocktail incorporating 2 to 3 measures of alcoholic ingredients makes a reasonably strong drink for one person. Cocktails with 4 or more measures are best made for two or more people.

## Atty

- ⚫⚫ dry gin
- ⚫ pastis
- ⚫ dry vermouth
- 2 dashes crème de violette

*Shake over ice. Strain into a cocktail glass.*

## Aviation

- ⚫⚫ dry gin
- ⚫ lemon juice
- 2 dashes maraschino

*Shake over ice. Strain into a cocktail glass.*

## Aviator

- ⚫ dry gin
- ⚫ dry vermouth
- ⚫ sweet vermouth
- ⚫ Dubonnet

*Shake over ice. Strain into a cocktail glass.*

## Banger

- ⚫⚫ dry gin
- ⚫ sweet vermouth
- 2 dashes Angostura bitters

*Stir over ice. Strain into a cocktail glass.*

## Banjino

- ⚫ dry gin
- ⚫ orange juice
- dash banana liqueur

*Shake over ice. Strain into a cocktail glass.*

## Barfly

- ⚫ dry gin
- ⚫ rum
- ⚫ pineapple juice

*Shake over ice. Strain into a cocktail glass.*

## Baron

∎∎ dry gin

∎ triple sec

∎ dry vermouth

teaspoon sweet vermouth

*Stir over ice. Strain into a cocktail glass and squeeze lemon peel over.*

## Bartender

∎ dry gin

∎ dry vermouth

∎ Dubonnet

∎ sherry

2 dashes Grand Marnier

*Stir over ice. Strain into a cocktail glass.*

## Beauty Spot

∎∎ dry gin

∎ dry vermouth

∎ sweet vermouth

teaspoon orange juice

dash grenadine

*Shake all but the grenadine over ice. Drop grenadine into a cocktail glass and then add the mix.*

## Beaux Arts

∎ dry gin

∎ dry vermouth

∎ sweet vermouth

∎ Amer Picon bitters

∎ Forbidden Fruit

*Stir over ice. Strain into a cocktail glass.*

## Belmont

∎∎ dry gin

∎ grenadine

teaspoon fresh cream

*Shake over ice. Strain into a cocktail glass.*

## Bennett

∎∎∎ dry gin

∎ fresh lime juice

2 dashes Angostura bitters

*Shake over ice. Strain into a cocktail glass.*

# Berlin

- ⚹ dry gin
- ⚹ madeira
- ⚹ orange juice

*Shake over ice. Strain into a cocktail glass.*

# Bermuda Bloom

- ⚹⚹ dry gin
- ⚹ apricot brandy
- ⚹⚹ lemon juice
- ⚹⚹ orange juice

3 dashes Cointreau

teaspoon sugar

*Shake over ice. Strain into ice-filled tall glasses.*

# Bermuda Pink

- ⚹⚹ dry gin
- ⚹ apricot brandy

teaspoon grenadine

*Shake over ice. Strain into a cocktail glass.*

# Berry Wall

- ⚹ dry gin
- ⚹ sweet vermouth

2 dashes curaçao

*Stir over ice. Strain into a cocktail glass.*

# Bich's Special

- ⚹⚹ dry gin
- ⚹ Lillet

dash Angostura bitters

*Shake over ice. Strain into a cocktail glass and add an orange slice.*

# Biffy

- ⚹⚹ dry gin
- ⚹ Swedish Punsch
- ⚹ lemon juice

*Shake over ice, Strain into a cocktail glass.*

---

You will find me drinking gin
In the lowest kind of inn.
Because I am a rigid Vegetarian.

G. K. Chesterton

## Bijou

- ▮ dry gin
- ▮ sweet vermouth
- ▮ green Chartreuse

dash orange bitters

*Stir over ice. Strain into a cocktail glass. Add maraschino cherry and lemon peel.*

## Biltong Dry

- ▮ dry gin
- ▮▮ Capéritif
- ▮ Dubonnet

dash orange bitters

*Stir over ice. Strain into a cocktail glass.*

## Biter

- ▮▮ dry gin
- ▮ green Chartreuse
- ▮ lemon juice

dash pastis

pinch sugar

*Shake over ice. Strain into a cocktail glass.*

## Blenton

- ▮▮ dry gin
- ▮ dry vermouth

dash Angostura bitters

*Stir over ice. Strain into a cocktail glass.*

## Bloodhound

- ▮▮ chilled dry gin
- ▮ chilled dry vermouth
- ▮ chilled sweet vermouth

3 chilled strawberries

*Put all ingredients into a blender and whizz. Pour into cocktail glasses.*

## Blue Bird

- ▮▮▮ dry gin
- ▮ orange curaçao

3 dashes Angostura bitters

*Stir over ice. Strain into cocktail glasses.*

## Bluebird

**∎ ∎** dry gin

**∎** dry vermouth

4 dashes cherry brandy

dash peach bitters

*Stir over ice. Strain into a cocktail glass. Add a maraschino cherry.*

## Blue Devil

**∎ ∎** dry gin

**∎** fresh lime (or lemon) juice

**∎** maraschino

dash blue food colouring

*Shake over ice. Strain into a cocktail glass.*

## Blue Moon

**∎ ∎** dry gin

**∎** blue curaçao

*Stir over ice. Strain into a cocktail glass.*

## Blue Train 2

**∎ ∎** dry gin

**∎** Cointreau

**∎** lemon juice

dash blue food colouring

*Shake over ice. Strain into a cocktail glass.*

## Boomerang

**∎ ∎ ∎** dry gin

**∎** dry vermouth

dash Angostura bitters

dash maraschino

*Stir over ice. Strain into a cocktail glass.*

## Breakfast

**∎ ∎** dry gin

**∎** grenadine

1 egg yolk

*Shake over ice. Strain into a small tumbler.*

---

Erma Bombeck, the American newspaper columnist, received a poisonous letter from a reader who did not like her waspish style. He ended with the phrase: 'I was married to a shrew like you once for three days.' She replied with brevity: 'How did you last so long?' He riposted in kind: 'I drank.'

## Bridal

▪▪ dry gin

▪ sweet vermouth

dash maraschino

dash orange bitters

*Shake over ice. Strain into a cocktail glass.*

## British Festival

▪▪ dry gin

▪ Drambuie

▪ fresh lime juice

*Shake over ice. Strain into a cocktail glass.*

## Bronx

▪▪▪ dry gin

▪ dry vermouth

▪ sweet vermouth

▪ orange juice

*Shake over ice. Strain into cocktail glasses.*

*For a 'Bronx Dry' substitute the sweet vermouth for an extra measure of dry vermouth.*

## Bronx Empress

▪ dry gin

▪ dry vermouth

▪ orange juice

2 dashes pastis

*Shake over ice. Strain into a cocktail glass.*

## Bronx River

▪▪ dry gin

▪ sweet vermouth

▪ lemon juice

sprinkling of sugar

*Shake over ice. Strain into cocktail glasses.*

## Bronx Silver

▪▪ dry gin

▪ dry vermouth

▪ orange juice

1 egg white

*Shake over ice. Strain into cocktail glasses.*

## Bronx Terrace

- ▮▮ dry gin
- ▮ dry vermouth
- ▮ fresh lime juice

*Shake over ice. Strain into a cocktail glass.*

## Brown

- ▮ dry gin
- ▮ white rum
- ▮ dry vermouth

*Stir over ice. Strain into a cocktail glass.*

## Bulldog 2

- ▮ dry gin
- ▮▮ orange juice
- chilled dry ginger ale

*Stir gin and orange juice in an ice-filled tumbler. Top up with ginger ale.*

## Butler

- ▮▮ dry gin
- ▮ pineapple juice
- 3 dashes apricot brandy

*Shake over ice. Strain into a cocktail glass.*

## Cabaret

- ▮ dry gin
- ▮ Capéritif
- dash pastis
- dash Angostura bitters

*Stir over ice. Strain into a cocktail glass and add a cocktail cherry.*

---

The ▮ symbol in the recipes is a 'unit' to indicate proportions. A reasonable single measure to use in mixing is about an ounce – equivalent to 30 millilitres (ml). Quantities in the recipes given as dashes, spoonfuls etc., are based on one-ounce unit measures of the accompanying principal ingredients. A cocktail incorporating 2 to 3 measures of alcoholic ingredients makes a reasonably strong drink for one person. Cocktails with 4 or more measures are best made for two or more people.

## Café de Paris

**‖** dry gin

3 dashes Anisette

teaspoon fresh cream

1 egg white

*Shake over ice. Strain into a cocktail glass.*

## Campden

**‖** dry gin

**▮** Cointreau

**▮** Lillet

*Stir over ice. Strain into a cocktail glass.*

## Cape

**▮** dry gin

**▮** Capéritif

**▮** orange juice

*Shake over ice. Strain into a cocktail glass.*

## Caruso

**▮** dry gin

**▮** dry vermouth

**▮** crème de menthe

*Stir over ice. Strain into a cocktail glass.*

## Casino

**‖** dry gin

2 dashes maraschino

2 dashes lemon juice

dash orange bitters

*Shake over ice. Strain into a cocktail glass and add a maraschino cherry.*

## Cat's Eye

**‖‖** dry gin

**‖▮** dry vermouth

**▮** Cointreau

**▮** kirsch

**▮** lemon juice

**▮** water

*Shake over ice. Strain into cocktail glasses.*

## CFH

**‖** dry gin

**▮** apple brandy

**▮** Swedish Punsch

**▮** grenadine

**▮** lemon juice

*Shake over ice. Strain into a cocktail glass.*

## Chanticleer

- ▮▮ dry gin
- ▮ lemon juice
- ▮ raspberry syrup
- 1 egg white

*Shake over ice. Strain into a cocktail glass.*

## Charleston

- ▮ dry gin
- ▮ kirsch
- ▮ curaçao
- ▮ dry vermouth
- ▮ sweet vermouth
- ▮ maraschino

*Shake over ice. Strain into a cocktail glass.*

## Chauffeur

- ▮ dry gin
- ▮ dry vermouth
- ▮ whisky
- dash Angostura bitters

*Shake over ice. Strain into a cocktail glass.*

*Invention of author and cocktail enthusiast H. E. Bates in* The Darling Buds of May, *1958.*

## Chelsea Arts

- ▮ dry gin
- ▮ Cointreau
- teaspoon lemon juice

*Shake over ice. Strain into a cocktail glass.*

## Cherry Cobbler

- ▮▮ dry gin
- ▮ cherry brandy
- ▮ lemon juice
- teaspoon sugar

*Pour ingredients into a tall, ice-filled glass and stir. Add a lemon slice and a maraschino cherry.*

## Church Parade

- ▮▮ dry gin
- ▮ dry vermouth
- ▮ orange juice
- dash orange bitters

*Shake over ice. Strain into a cocktail glass.*

## Claridge

- ⠶ dry gin
- ⠿ dry vermouth
- ⠿ Cointreau
- ⠿ apricot brandy

*Stir over ice. Strain into cocktail glasses.*

## Clover Club

- ⠶ dry gin
- ⠿ grenadine
- ⠿ fresh lime juice
- 1 egg white

*Shake over ice. Strain into a cocktail glass.*

## Clover Leaf

- ⠶ dry gin
- ⠿ grenadine
- ⠿ fresh lime juice
- 1 egg white

*Shake over ice. Strain into a cocktail glass. Add mint sprig to glass.*

## Club

- ⠶ dry gin
- ⠿ sweet vermouth
- dash yellow Chartreuse

*Stir over ice. Strain into a cocktail glass.*

## Cobbler

- ⠶ dry gin
- teaspoon caster sugar

*Fill a tumbler with ice. Sprinkle sugar over. Add gin. Decorate with fruit slices.*

*This American-inspired cocktail can be made with any type of spirit.*

## Colonial

- ⠶ dry gin
- ⠿ grapefruit juice
- 3 dashes maraschino

*Shake over ice. Strain into a cocktail glass.*

---

To provoke or sustain a reverie in a bar you have to drink English gin, especially in the form of the dry martini.

Luis Buñuel

## Comet

- ✷ dry gin
- 4 dashes Strega
- 4 dashes Van der Hum

*Stir over ice. Strain into cocktail glasses and add lemon peel.*

## Cooperstown

- ✷ dry gin
- ✷ dry vermouth
- ✷ sweet vermouth

*Stir over ice. Strain into a cocktail glass and add a mint sprig.*

## Copenhagen

- ✷ ✷ ✷ dry gin
- ✷ aquavit
- 3 dashes dry vermouth

*Stir over ice. Strain into cocktail glasses.*

## Cordova

- ✷ ✷ dry gin
- ✷ sweet vermouth
- dash pastis
- teaspoon fresh cream

*Shake over ice. Strain into a cocktail glass.*

## Cornell

- ✷ ✷ dry gin
- 4 dashes maraschino
- 2 dashes lemon juice
- 1 egg white

*Shake over ice. Strain into a cocktail glass.*

## Corpse Reviver

- ✷ dry gin
- ✷ Cointreau
- ✷ Lillet
- ✷ lemon juice
- dash pastis

*Shake over ice. Strain into a cocktail glass.*

*Recommended the night before rather than the morning after.*

## Crimson

- ▪▪ dry gin
- ▪ port
- ▪ lemon juice
- 3 dashes grenadine

*Shake the gin, lemon and grenadine over ice. Strain into a small wine glass and pour the port gently over.*

## Damn the Weather

- ▪▪ dry gin
- ▪ sweet vermouth
- ▪ orange juice
- 3 dashes curaçao

*Shake over ice. Strain into cocktail glasses.*

## D'Amour

- ▪▪ dry gin
- ▪ Anisette
- ▪ fresh lime juice
- 1 egg white

*Shake over ice. Strain into a cocktail glass.*

## Débutante

- ▪▪ dry gin
- ▪ crème de noyaux
- ▪▪ lemon juice
- ▪ lime juice

*Shake over ice. Strain into a cocktail glass.*

## Deep Sea

- ▪ dry gin
- ▪ dry vermouth
- dash pastis
- dash orange bitters

*Stir over ice. Strain into a cocktail glass.*

## Delmonico

- ▪▪▪ dry gin
- ▪ brandy
- ▪ dry vermouth
- ▪ sweet vermouth
- dash Angostura bitters

*Stir over ice. Strain into cocktail glasses.*

## Dempsey

- ⬥ dry gin
- ⬥ apple brandy
- 4 dashes pastis
- 2 dashes grenadine

*Stir over ice. Strain into a cocktail glass.*

## Depth Charge

- ⬥ dry gin
- ⬥ Lillet
- 2 dashes pastis

*Stir over ice. Strain into a cocktail glass.*

## Derby

- ⬥ dry gin
- 2 dashes peach bitters
- 2 mint sprigs

*Shake over ice. Strain into a cocktail glass.*

## Desert Healer

- ⬥ dry gin
- ⬥ fresh orange juice
- 3 dashes cherry brandy

*Shake over ice. Strain into a cocktail glass.*

## Devonia

- ⬥ dry gin
- ⬥⬥ sparkling cider
- dash orange bitters

*Shake, gently, over ice. Strain into a cocktail glass.*

## Dixie

- ⬥⬥ dry gin
- ⬥ dry vermouth
- ⬥ pastis

*Stir over ice. Strain into cocktail glasses.*

---

The ⬥ symbol in the recipes is a 'unit' to indicate proportions. A reasonable single measure to use in mixing is about an ounce – equivalent to 30 millilitres (ml). Quantities in the recipes given as dashes, spoonfuls etc., are based on one-ounce unit measures of the accompanying principal ingredients. A cocktail incorporating 2 to 3 measures of alcoholic ingredients makes a reasonably strong drink for one person. Cocktails with 4 or more measures are best made for two or more people.

## Dog's Nose

- **x** dry gin
- glass of beer

*Add the gin to the beer.*

*A 'sly-grog' concoction once widely enjoyed in the wardrooms of Royal Navy ships.*

## Dolly Hoskins

- **xxx** dry gin
- **xx** peach brandy
- **x** fresh cream
- 4 dashes grenadine

*Shake over ice. Strain into cocktail glasses.*

## Dolly O'Dare

- **xx** dry gin
- **xx** dry vermouth
- **x** apricot brandy

*Stir over ice. Strain into cocktail glasses.*

## Dry Martini

*See Martini*

## Dubarry

- **xx** dry gin
- **x** dry vermouth
- 4 dashes pastis
- 2 dashes Angostura bitters

*Stir over ice. Strain into a cocktail glass.*

## Eagle's Dream

- **xxx** dry gin
- **x** Crème Yvette
- teaspoon sugar
- 1 egg white

*Shake over ice. Strain into cocktail glasses.*

## Eclipse

- **x** dry gin
- **x** sloe gin
- teaspoon grenadine

*Shake gins over ice. Strain into a cocktail glass containing the grenadine. Squeeze orange peel over.*

## Eddie Brown

- ▮ dry gin
- ▮ Lillet
- 2 dashes apricot brandy

*Stir over ice. Strain into a cocktail glass.*

## Elk

- ▮ dry gin
- ▮ prunelle liqueur
- 2 dashes dry vermouth

*Stir over ice. Strain into a cocktail glass.*

## Emerald Isle

- ▮▮ dry gin
- teaspoon green crème de menthe
- dash Angostura bitters

*Stir over ice. Strain into a cocktail glass.*

## Empire

- ▮▮ dry gin
- ▮ apple brandy
- ▮ apricot brandy

*Stir over ice. Strain into cocktail glasses.*

## English Rose

- ▮▮ dry gin
- ▮▮ dry vermouth
- ▮ apricot brandy
- 4 dashes grenadine
- dash lemon juice

*Shake over ice. Strain into cocktail glasses.*

## Eton Blazer

- ▮▮▮ dry gin
- ▮ kirsch
- ▮ lemon juice
- teaspoon sugar

*Shake over ice. Strain into cocktail glasses.*

## Fairbanks Senior

- ▮ dry gin
- ▮ dry vermouth
- dash crème de menthe
- dash orange bitters

*Stir over ice. Strain into cocktail glasses.*

## Fairy Belle

✿ ✿ ✿ dry gin

✿ apricot brandy

teaspoon grenadine

1 egg white

*Shake over ice. Strain into cocktail glasses.*

## Fallen Angel

✿ ✿ dry gin

✿ lemon juice

2 dashes crème de menthe

dash Angostura bitters

*Shake over ice. Strain into a cocktail glass.*

## Fare Thee Well

✿ ✿ ✿ dry gin

✿ dry vermouth

4 dashes sweet vermouth

dash lemon juice

*Shake over ice. Strain into cocktail glasses.*

## Farmer

✿ ✿ dry gin

✿ dry vermouth

✿ sweet vermouth

2 dashes orange bitters

*Stir over ice. Strain into cocktail glasses.*

## Fascinator

✿ ✿ dry gin

✿ dry vermouth

2 dashes pastis

sprig fresh mint

*Shake over ice. Strain into a cocktail glass.*

## Fifty-Fifty

✿ dry gin

✿ dry vermouth

*Stir over ice. Strain into a cocktail glass and add a cocktail olive.*

*This is the original 'martini'. See entry.*

---

Gin's cheap. It hits.

Raymond Chandler,
*Farewell My Lovely*

## Fine and Dandy

- ▮▮ dry gin
- ▮ Cointreau
- ▮ lemon juice

dash Angostura bitters

*Stir over ice. Strain into cocktail glasses.*

## Finotini

- ▮▮▮ dry gin
- ▮ fino (pale, dry) sherry

*Shake over ice. Strain into cocktail glasses and squeeze lemon peel over.*

## 5757 Gin Margarita

- ▮▮▮ dry gin
- ▮▮ lemon juice, sweetened to taste
- ▮ Cointreau

*Shake over ice. Strain into cocktail glasses.*

*Recipe of Fifty-Seven-Fifty-Seven bar in Four Seasons Hotel, New York City.*

## Flamingo

- ▮▮▮ dry gin
- ▮ apricot brandy
- ▮ fresh lime juice

teaspoon grenadine

*Shake gin, brandy and lime over ice. Strain into ice-filled tumblers and stir in grenadine.*

## Floradora

- ▮▮ dry gin
- ▮ fresh lime juice

teaspoon grenadine

teaspoon caster sugar

chilled dry ginger ale

*Shake first four ingredients over ice. Strain into a tall, ice-filled glass, top with ginger ale and stir.*

## Florida

- ▮ dry gin

teaspoon Cointreau

teaspoon kirsch

- ▮▮▮ orange juice

2 dashes lemon juice

*Shake over ice. Strain into cocktail glasses.*

## Flying Dutchman

    ▮ genever (Dutch gin)

    dash Cointreau

    dash orange bitters

*Stir over ice. Strain into a
cocktail glass.*

## Fog Horn

    ▮▮ dry gin

    ▮ fresh lime juice

    chilled dry ginger ale

*Pour gin and lime into an ice-
filled tumbler. Top with ginger
ale and add a lime slice.*

## Frankenjack

    ▮▮ dry gin

    ▮▮ dry vermouth

    ▮ apricot brandy

    ▮ Cointreau

*Stir over ice. Strain into
cocktail glasses.*

## French Rose

    ▮▮ dry gin

    ▮ cherry brandy

    ▮ dry vermouth

*Stir over ice. Strain into
cocktail glasses.*

---

The great comedian and epic drinker W. C. Fields (1879–1946) was
in the habit of carrying an enormous flask of spirit with him on film
sets. He assured the studio bosses, who frowned on drinking, that
the flask contained nothing more than pineapple juice, and they
chose to believe him. But on one occasion, a couple of fellow actors
managed to purloin the flask – and to fill it with real pineapple juice.
When Fields, unawares, took his next swig between takes, his
outburst entered Hollywood legend: 'Somebody's been putting
pineapple juice in my pineapple juice.'

*Spyglass*

# French 75

∎∎ Plymouth gin

∎ fresh lime juice

chilled sparkling wine

*Shake gin and lime over ice.*
*Strain into small wine glasses*
*and top with sparkling wine.*
*Add a maraschino cherry.*

# Froth Blower

∎∎∎∎ dry gin

∎ grenadine

1 egg white

*Shake over ice. Strain into*
*cocktail glasses.*

# Gasper

∎ dry gin

∎ pastis

*Stir over ice. Strain into a*
*cocktail glass.*

# Gazebo

∎∎∎ dry gin

∎ Cointreau

∎ blue curaçao

dash Angostura bitters

*Stir over ice. Strain into small,*
*ice-filled wine glasses.*

# Gene Tunney

∎ dry gin

∎ dry vermouth

dash lemon juice

dash orange juice

*Shake over ice. Strain into a*
*cocktail glass.*

# Gibson

∎ dry gin

dash dry vermouth

*Stir over ice. Strain into a*
*cocktail glass. Squeeze lemon*
*peel over and add a cocktail*
*onion.*

*A variation on the dry martini*
*– the variant being the onion.*

# Gimlet

∎ dry gin

∎ lime juice cordial

*Pour over ice in a cocktail*
*glass.*

*Said to be named after naval*
*surgeon Sir T. O. Gimlette*
*who devised the drink in 1890.*
*He believed the addition of*
*lime juice made for a healthier*
*drink for ships' officers in the*
*habit of taking their gin neat.*

## Gin and Cape

- ✶ dry gin
- ✶ Capéritif

*Stir over ice. Strain into a cocktail glass.*

## Gin and It

- ✶ dry gin
- ✶ sweet vermouth

*Stir over ice. Strain into a cocktail glass.*

*In effect, a sweet martini. The 'It' is a contraction of Italian.*

## Gin Cocktail

- ✶ dry gin
- 2 dashes orange bitters

*Shake over ice. Strain into a cocktail glass.*

## Gin Daisy

- ✶ dry gin
- ✶ lemon juice
- teaspoon grenadine
- sprinkling of sugar

*Shake over ice. Strain into an ice-filled tall glass and add orange and lemon slices.*

## Gin Fix

- ✶ dry gin
- ✶ lemon juice
- tablespoon sugar syrup

*Mix lemon and syrup in a tumbler before adding ice. Pour gin over and add a lemon slice.*

---

I never drink gin. It makes me by turns bellicose, lachrymose and comatose.

Elisabeth, Lady Clapham

## Gin Fizz

∎∎ dry gin

∎ lemon juice

teaspoon sugar

soda water

*Shake first three ingredients over ice. Strain into a small wine glass and top with soda.*

## Gin Rickey

∎∎ dry gin

∎ fresh lime juice

chilled sparkling water

*Pour gin and lime into an ice-filled tall glass. Top with sparkling water and add a maraschino cherry.*

## Ginsin

∎ dry gin

∎ grapefruit juice

∎ orange juice

dash grenadine

*Shake over ice. Strain into a cocktail glass and add a strawberry.*

## Gin Sling

∎ dry gin

teaspoon sugar syrup

chilled soda water

*Add gin and sugar to a tall tumbler containing ice cubes. Top with soda.*

*As a hot drink, substitute boiling water for soda and add a pinch of nutmeg.*

## Glass Slipper

∎∎∎ dry gin

∎ blue curaçao

*Stir over ice. Strain into a cocktail glass.*

## Glider

∎∎∎ dry gin

∎ fresh lime juice

2 dashes grenadine

dash pastis

1 egg white

*Shake over ice. Strain into cocktail glasses.*

## Golden Gate

▮ dry gin

▮▮▮ frozen orange juice

*Shake vigorously. Strain into cocktail glasses.*

## Golf

▮▮ dry gin

▮ dry vermouth

dash Angostura bitters

*Stir over ice. Strain into a cocktail glass.*

## Good Night Ladies

▮▮▮ dry gin

▮ apricot brandy

▮ grenadine

▮ lemon juice

*Shake over ice. Strain into cocktail glasses.*

## Gordon Bennett

▮▮ Gordon's gin

▮ cider brandy

▮ dry vermouth

teaspoon lemon juice

*Shake over ice and strain into a cocktail glass.*

Gordon Bennett, once New York's most eligible bachelor, is commemorated in a cocktail. His name has been adopted, too, as a Cockney expletive, expressing outrage or disbelief. Bennett was thus immortalised by getting very drunk before calling upon his fiancée at her home to discuss their wedding arrangements. Entering the drawing room where his intended's family was gathered, the young man became disoriented – and mistook the fireplace for a plumbing appliance. The marriage was called off and the heir to one of America's greatest fortunes fled to Europe to escape the scandal. In one edition of the *Guinness Book of Records*, this incident was described as 'the most expensive *faux pas* in history' because of the loss of revenue to the US Treasury of taxes from the exiled Bennett millions.

## Grand Passion

- ▮▮ dry gin
- ▮ passionfruit juice
- dash Angostura bitters

*Shake over ice. Strain into a cocktail glass.*

## Grand Royal Clover Club

- ▮▮ dry gin
- ▮ grenadine
- ▮ lemon juice
- 1 egg

*Shake over ice. Strain into cocktail glasses.*

## Grapefruit

- ▮▮ dry gin
- ▮ grapefruit juice

*Shake over ice. Strain into a cocktail glass.*

## Grape Vine

- ▮▮ dry gin
- ▮ grape juice
- ▮ lemon juice
- dash grenadine

*Shake over ice. Strain into cocktail glasses.*

## Great Secret

- ▮▮ dry gin
- ▮ Lillet
- dash Angostura bitters

*Stir over ice. Strain into a cocktail glass.*

## Green Dragon

- ▮▮ dry gin
- ▮ Green Mint
- ▮ kümmel
- ▮ lemon juice
- 4 dashes peach bitters

*Shake over ice. Strain into cocktail glasses.*

## Green Lady

- ▮▮ dry gin
- ▮ green Chartreuse
- 4 dashes fresh lime juice

*Shake over ice. Strain into a cocktail glass.*

## Guard's

- ▮▮ dry gin
- ▮ sweet vermouth
- 2 dashes curaçao

*Stir over ice. Strain into cocktail glasses.*

## H & H

- ▮▮ dry gin
- ▮ Lillet
- 2 dashes curaçao

*Stir over ice. Strain into a cocktail glass.*

## Hakam

- ▮ dry gin
- ▮ sweet vermouth
- 2 dashes curaçao
- dash orange bitters

*Stir over ice. Strain into a cocktail glass.*

## Hanky Panky

- ▮ dry gin
- ▮ sweet vermouth
- 2 dashes Fernet Branca

*Stir over ice. Strain into a cocktail glass and squeeze orange peel over.*

## Happy Return

- ▮▮▮▮ dry gin
- ▮▮ Cointreau
- ▮ cherry brandy
- teaspoon lemon juice

*Shake over ice. Strain into cocktail glasses. Add maraschino cherries.*

---

The ▮ symbol in the recipes is a 'unit' to indicate proportions. A reasonable single measure to use in mixing is about an ounce – equivalent to 30 millilitres (ml). Quantities in the recipes given as dashes, spoonfuls etc., are based on one-ounce unit measures of the accompanying principal ingredients. A cocktail incorporating 2 to 3 measures of alcoholic ingredients makes a reasonably strong drink for one person. Cocktails with 4 or more measures are best made for two or more people.

## Harlem

- ▪▪ dry gin
- ▪ pineapple juice
- 2 dashes maraschino

*Shake over ice. Strain into a cocktail glass.*

## Harrovian

- ▪ dry gin
- 2 dashes orange juice
- dash lemon juice

*Shake over ice. Strain into a cocktail glass.*

## Harry's

- ▪▪ dry gin
- ▪ sweet vermouth
- dash pastis
- 2 sprigs fresh mint

*Stir over ice. Strain into a cocktail glass and add a cocktail olive.*

## Hasty

- ▪▪ dry gin
- ▪ dry vermouth
- 4 dashes grenadine
- dash pastis

*Stir over ice. Strain into a cocktail glass.*

## Hawaiian

- ▪▪ dry gin
- ▪ curaçao
- ▪ orange juice

*Shake over ice. Strain into cocktail glasses.*

## High Flyer

- ▪▪▪ dry gin
- ▪ Strega
- 3 dashes Van der Hum

*Stir over ice. Strain into cocktail glasses.*

---

I have been drinking very heavily since I was 14 and now my palate has been so destroyed, I'm afraid, that the other night I drank a whole bottle of what I thought was tequila and didn't realise until the next day that it was Strega.

Julie Burchill, *The Spectator*, 1992

# Hokkaido

∎∎∎ dry gin

∎∎ sake

∎ Cointreau

*Stir over ice. Strain into cocktail glasses.*

# Holland House

∎∎ dry gin

∎ dry vermouth

∎ lemon juice

4 dashes maraschino

slice pineapple

*Shake over ice. Strain into cocktail glasses.*

# Homestead

∎∎ dry gin

∎ sweet vermouth

slice orange

*Shake over ice. Strain into a cocktail glass.*

# Honolulu

∎ dry gin

dash Angostura bitters

2 dashes lemon juice

dash orange juice

dash pineapple juice

*Shake over ice. Strain into a cocktail glass.*

# Hula-Hula

∎∎ dry gin

∎ fresh orange juice

dash Cointreau

*Shake over ice. Strain into a cocktail glass.*

# Ideal

∎∎ dry gin

∎ dry vermouth

∎ grapefruit juice

2 dashes maraschino

*Shake over ice. Strain into cocktail glasses. Add a blanched almond.*

## Imperial

- dry gin
- dry vermouth

dash Angostura bitters

dash maraschino

*Stir over ice. Strain into a cocktail glass. Add a cocktail olive.*

## Inca

- dry gin
- dry sherry
- dry vermouth
- sweet vermouth

dash Orgeat syrup

dash orange bitters

*Stir over ice. Strain into cocktail glasses.*

When his mother died in 1822, Hertfordshire landowner James Lucas locked himself in the kitchen of his home with her corpse – and remained there for twenty-five years. He subsisted on a diet of bread and cheese, eggs and herrings. And gin. He never left the kitchen (his mother was forcefully removed to the family vault by police) but received visitors. Most were vagrants, whom he plied with gin in exchange for news of events in the outside world. Celebrity callers included Charles Dickens, who immortalised Lucas as 'that obscene nuisance', Mr Mopes.

Lucas was fond of children, and each Good Friday held a party for them. Every child was given a bag of sweets, a penny and a glass of gin.

When Lucas died in 1847, the ash, rubbish and empty gin bottles from his long kitchen sojourn came to fourteen cartloads.

## Income Tax

▮▮▮ dry gin

▮▮ orange juice

▮ equal mix sweet and dry vermouth

dash Angostura bitters

*Shake over ice and strain into cocktail glasses.*

## Jabberwock

▮ dry gin

▮ Capéritif

▮ dry sherry

2 dashes orange bitters

*Stir over ice. Strain into a cocktail glass.*

## Jack Kearns

▮▮▮ dry gin

▮ rum

dash lemon juice

dash sugar syrup

*Shake over ice. Strain into cocktail glasses.*

## Jack Pine

▮▮ dry gin

▮ dry vermouth

▮ orange juice

slice pineapple

*Shake over ice. Strain into cocktail glasses.*

## Jamaica Sunset

▮▮▮ dry gin

▮ dark rum

▮ red wine

▮ orange juice

*Shake over ice. Strain into cocktail glasses.*

## Java Cooler

▮▮ dry gin

4 dashes fresh lime juice

dash Angostura bitters

chilled tonic water

*Pour gin, lime and bitters over ice in a tall glass. Top up with tonic and stir.*

# Jewel

- ▪ dry gin
- ▪ sweet vermouth
- ▪ green Chartreuse
- 2 dashes orange bitters

*Stir over ice. Strain into a cocktail glass and add a maraschino cherry.*

# Jeyplack

- ▪▪ dry gin
- ▪ sweet vermouth
- dash pastis

*Stir over ice. Strain into a cocktail glass and squeeze lemon peel over.*

# Jimmy Blanc

- ▪▪ dry gin
- ▪ Lillet
- 3 dashes Dubonnet

*Stir over ice. Strain into a cocktail glass and squeeze orange peel over.*

# Jockey Club

- ▪ dry gin
- teaspoon lemon juice
- 2 dashes crème de noyaux
- dash Angostura bitters
- dash orange bitters

*Shake over ice. Strain into a cocktail glass.*

# John Collins

- ▪▪ Dutch gin
- ▪ lemon juice
- teaspoon sugar
- soda water

*Shake gin, juice and sugar over ice. Strain into a tall, ice-filled glass and top with soda.*

# J.O.S.

- ▪ dry gin
- ▪ dry vermouth
- ▪ sweet vermouth
- dash brandy
- dash lemon juice
- dash orange bitters

*Shake over ice. Strain into a cocktail glass.*

## Joulouville

- ▮▮ dry gin
- ▮ apple brandy
- ▮ sweet vermouth
- teaspoon lemon juice
- dash grenadine

*Shake over ice. Strain into cocktail glasses.*

## Journalist

- ▮▮ dry gin
- ▮ dry vermouth
- ▮ sweet vermouth
- 2 dashes curaçao
- 2 dashes lemon juice
- dash Angostura bitters

*Shake over ice. Strain into cocktail glasses.*

## Judgette

- ▮ dry gin
- ▮ dry vermouth
- ▮ peach brandy
- dash lime cordial

*Shake over ice. Strain into a cocktail glass.*

## Jupiter

- ▮▮▮ dry gin
- ▮▮ dry vermouth
- ▮ Parfait Amour
- ▮ orange juice

*Shake over ice. Strain into cocktail glasses.*

## KCB

- ▮▮▮ dry gin
- ▮ kirsch
- dash apricot brandy
- dash lemon juice

*Shake over ice. Strain into cocktail glasses.*

## KGB

- ▮▮▮ dry gin
- ▮ kümmel
- 3 dashes apricot brandy
- 3 dashes lemon juice

*Shake over ice. Strain into cocktail glasses.*

# Kina

- ⬤⬤ dry gin
- ⬤ Lillet
- ⬤ sweet vermouth

*Stir over ice. Strain into cocktail glasses.*

# Kiss Kiss

- ⬤ dry gin
- ⬤ cherry brandy
- ⬤ sweet vermouth

*Stir over ice. Strain into cocktail glasses.*

# Knickerbocker

- ⬤ dry gin
- ⬤ dry vermouth
- dash sweet vermouth

*Stir over ice. Strain into a cocktail glass and squeeze lemon peel over.*

# Knockout

- ⬤ dry gin
- ⬤ dry vermouth
- ⬤ pastis
- teaspoon white crème de menthe

*Stir over ice. Strain into a cocktail glass.*

# Kup's Indispensable

- ⬤⬤⬤ dry gin
- ⬤ dry vermouth
- 4 dashes sweet vermouth
- dash pastis

*Stir over ice. Strain into cocktail glasses and squeeze orange peel over.*

---

Gin and water is the source of all my inspiration.        Lord Byron

## Lady's Finger

- ▮▮ dry gin
- ▮ cherry brandy
- ▮ kirsch

*Stir over ice. Strain into cocktail glasses.*

## Lasky

- ▮ dry gin
- ▮ grape juice
- ▮ Swedish Punsch

*Shake over ice. Strain into a cocktail glass.*

## Leap Frog

- ▮ dry gin
- 4 dashes lemon juice
- dry ginger ale

*Pour gin and lemon over ice in a tumbler. Top with ginger ale.*

## Leap Year

- ▮▮▮▮ dry gin
- ▮ Grand Marnier
- ▮ sweet vermouth
- dash lemon juice

*Stir over ice. Strain into cocktail glasses.*

## Leave It To Me

- ▮ dry gin
- ▮ apricot brandy
- ▮ dry vermouth
- dash grenadine
- dash lemon juice

*Stir over ice. Strain into a cocktail glass.*

## Le Chanticleer

- ▮▮ dry gin
- ▮▮ lemon juice
- ▮ Bénédictine
- ▮ crème de noyaux

*Shake over ice. Strain into cocktail glasses.*

## Lily

- ▮ dry gin
- ▮ crème de noyaux
- ▮ Lillet
- dash lemon juice

*Shake over ice. Strain into a cocktail glass.*

## Little Devil

- ▮▮ dry gin
- ▮▮ rum
- ▮ Cointreau
- ▮ lemon juice

*Shake over ice. Strain into cocktail glasses.*

## Londino

- ▮ dry gin
- ▮ dry vermouth
- ▮ orange juice
- ▮ apricot brandy
- ▮ Campari

*Shake over ice. Strain into cocktail glasses.*

## London

- ▮ dry gin
- 2 dashes orange bitters
- 2 dashes pastis
- 2 dashes sugar syrup

*Shake over ice. Strain into a cocktail glass.*

## Lone Tree

- ▮ dry gin
- ▮ dry vermouth
- ▮ sweet vermouth
- 2 dashes orange bitters

*Stir over ice. Strain into a cocktail glass.*

---

The toast 'Here's mud in your eye' commemorates an unlucky American doctor. Samuel Mudd had a country practice near Washington, and one night in April 1865 was visited by a very excitable patient in his mid-fifties with a broken shin. He treated the man and thought no more of it until discovering the next day that President Abraham Lincoln had been assassinated. The killer's description matched that of his patient. Dr Mudd contacted the authorities at once, but to his dismay was accused of conspiring with the assassin, John Wilkes Booth.

Mudd was imprisoned for life. His pleas of innocence were widely publicised (and ignored) and his name came to symbolise anyone who vigorously denied involvement in a crime, innocent or otherwise.

## Lone Tree Cooler

**✶** dry gin

**✶** soda water

teaspoon dry vermouth

pinch of caster sugar

extra soda water

*Stir the measure of soda and the sugar in a tall glass, and add ice. Next add the gin and vermouth. Finally top up the glass with soda and garnish with an orange slice.*

## Lord Suffolk

**✶** dry gin

4 dashes Cointreau

4 dashes maraschino

4 dashes sweet vermouth

*Stir over ice. Strain into a cocktail glass.*

## Lorraine

**✶✶** dry gin

**✶** Grand Marnier

**✶** Lillet

*Stir over ice. Strain into a cocktail glass.*

## Luigi

**✶✶** dry gin

**✶✶** dry vermouth

**✶** tangerine juice

2 dashes grenadine

dash Cointreau

*Shake over ice. Strain into cocktail glasses.*

## Magnolia Blossom

**✶✶** dry gin

**✶** fresh cream

**✶** lemon juice

*Shake over ice. Strain into a cocktail glass.*

## Mahjongg

**✶✶✶✶** dry gin

**✶** Cointreau

**✶** rum

*Stir over ice. Strain into cocktail glasses.*

## Maiden's Blush (1)

**▪▪** dry gin

**▪** pastis

2 dashes grenadine

*Stir over ice. Strain into a cocktail glass.*

## Maiden's Blush (2)

**▪▪▪▪** dry gin

**▪** orange curaçao

**▪** grenadine

dash lemon juice

*Shake over ice. Strain into cocktail glasses.*

## Maiden's Prayer

**▪** dry gin

**▪** Cointreau

teaspoon lemon juice

teaspoon orange juice

*Shake over ice. Strain into a cocktail glass.*

## Manhasset Mauler

**▪▪** dry gin

**▪** sloe gin

*Shake over ice. Strain into a cocktail glass and squeeze lemon peel over.*

## Marmalade

**▪▪** dry gin

**▪** lemon juice

teaspoon marmalade

*Shake over ice. Strain into a cocktail glass and squeeze orange peel over.*

## Marny

**▪▪** dry gin

**▪** Grand Marnier

*Stir over ice. Strain into a cocktail glass.*

## Martinez

**▪** dry gin

teaspoon curaçao

dash orange bitters

*Stir over ice. Strain into a cocktail glass and add a maraschino cherry and lemon peel.*

## Martini

**&** dry gin

teaspoon dry vermouth

*Stir over ice. Strain into a cocktail glass and squeeze lemon peel over.*

*The variable 'dryness' of a martini is determined by the proportion of vermouth to gin. A Medium Martini is made with one part vermouth to two gin. A Dry Martini is commonly understood to be one part vermouth to four gin. An Extra Dry Martini is one part vermouth to eight parts gin. To make an Ultra Dry Martini stir one part vermouth over ice, then drain it off and stir four parts gin over the same ice and strain into a cocktail glass.*

*The original martini was made with equal measures of vermouth and gin by Martini de Arma de Taggia, barman at the Knickerbocker Hotel in New York City around 1900. The vermouth used was very likely (but coincidentally) a brand of Martini & Rossi of Turin, Italy.*

A lady wearing a very low-cut dress took a stool at a New York cocktail bar.

'Hey, burman,' she told the barman, 'Gimme a martoni.'

The barman mixed her a dry martini. She drank it at once and demanded another one. After a third, she lit a cheroot, leaned across the bar and said to the barman: 'What are you putting in those martonis, burman? They're giving me heartboyn.'

The barman sighed. 'Look, lady. I ain't a burman. I'm a barman. And they ain't martonis; they're martinis. And you ain't got heartboyn. You've got your cleavage in the ashtray.'

## Matinee

- ▮▮ dry gin
- ▮ Sambuca
- ▮ fresh cream
- 4 dashes fresh lime juice
- 1 egg white

*Shake over ice. Strain into cocktail glasses.*

## Maurice

- ▮▮ dry gin
- ▮ dry vermouth
- ▮ sweet vermouth
- ▮ orange juice
- dash pastis

*Shake over ice. Strain into cocktail glasses.*

## Mayfair

- ▮▮ dry gin
- ▮ apricot brandy
- ▮ orange juice
- dash clove syrup

*Shake over ice. Strain into a cocktail glass.*

## Merry Widow 2

- ▮ dry gin
- ▮ dry vermouth
- 2 dashes Angostura bitters
- 2 dashes Bénédictine
- 2 dashes pastis

*Stir over ice. Strain into a cocktail glass.*

## Million Dollar

- ▮▮▮▮ dry gin
- ▮▮ sweet vermouth
- ▮ pineapple juice
- 2 dashes grenadine

*Shake over ice. Strain into cocktail glasses.*

## Mint Collins

- ▮▮ dry gin
- ▮ lemon juice
- teaspoon sugar
- chilled sparkling water
- 3 mint sprigs

*Crush two of the mint sprigs and place in a tall glass. Add ice cubes, followed by the gin, lemon and sugar. Top with sparkling water and add remaining mint sprig.*

## Modder River

- ∎∎ dry gin
- ∎ Capéritif
- ∎ dry vermouth

*Stir over ice. Strain into a cocktail glass.*

## Moll

- ∎ dry gin
- ∎ dry vermouth
- ∎ sloe gin
- dash orange bitters
- sprinkle sugar

*Shake over ice. Strain into a cocktail glass.*

## Monkey Brain

- ∎ dry gin
- ∎ Bénédictine
- ∎ lemon juice
- dash grenadine

*Shake over ice. Strain into a cocktail glass.*

## Monkey Gland

- ∎∎∎ dry gin
- ∎ orange juice
- 2 dashes pastis
- 2 dashes grenadine

*Shake over ice. Strain into cocktail glasses.*

## Monte Carlo Imperial

- ∎∎ dry gin
- ∎ white crème de menthe
- ∎ lemon juice
- chilled champagne

*Shake spirits and lemon over ice. Strain into a wine glass and top with champagne.*

## Montmartre

- ∎∎∎ dry gin
- ∎ Cointreau
- ∎ sweet vermouth

*Stir over ice. Strain into cocktail glasses.*

---

Not drunk is he who from the floor
Can rise alone and still drink more.
But drunk is he who prostrate lies
Without the power to drink or rise.

Thomas Love Peacock,
*The Misfortunes of Elphin*

## Moonlight

- ▮▮ dry gin
- ▮▮ white wine
- ▮ grapefruit juice
- 4 dashes kirsch

*Shake over ice. Strain into wine glasses and add a twist of lemon peel.*

## Morro

- ▮▮ dry gin
- ▮ rum
- ▮ fresh lime juice
- ▮ pineapple juice

*Shake over ice. Strain into cocktail glasses.*

## My Fair Lady

- ▮▮ dry gin
- ▮ orange juice
- ▮ lemon juice
- 3 dashes strawberry liqueur
- 1 egg white

*Shake over ice. Strain into cocktail glasses.*

## Napoleon

- ▮ dry gin
- dash curaçao
- dash Dubonnet
- dash Fernet Branca

*Stir over ice. Strain into a cocktail glass and squeeze lemon peel over.*

## Negroni

- ▮ dry gin
- ▮ Campari
- ▮ sweet vermouth

*Stir over ice. Strain into a cocktail glass.*

## New Arrival

- ▮ dry gin
- ▮ Grand Marnier
- 2 dashes Crème Yvette
- 2 dashes Lillet

*Stir over ice. Strain into a cocktail glass.*

## Newbury

- ⚫ dry gin
- ⚫ sweet vermouth
- 3 dashes curaçao
- strip lemon rind
- strip orange rind

*Shake over ice. Strain into a cocktail glass.*

## New Orleans Gin Fizz

- ⚫⚫ dry gin
- ⚫ fresh lime juice
- ⚫ lemon juice
- 1 egg white
- tablespoon cream
- teaspoon sugar
- chilled sparkling water

*Shake all but sparkling water over ice. Strain into ice-filled tall glasses and top with sparkling water.*

## Nineteenth Hole

- ⚫⚫⚫ dry gin
- ⚫⚫ dry vermouth
- ⚫ sweet vermouth
- dash Angostura bitters

*Stir over ice. Strain into cocktail glasses.*

## Noddy

- ⚫⚫⚫ dry gin
- ⚫⚫ bourbon
- ⚫ pastis

*Stir over ice. Strain into cocktail glasses.*

---

London became the capital of gin distilling by Act of Parliament in 1690 when King William III imposed punitive duties on imported spirits in order to encourage domestic production. Gin consumption in England increased from around half a million gallons in 1690 to 20 million gallons in 1751 when Parliament finally introduced enforcable domestic duties to reduce the resulting epidemic of alcoholism.

## Old Etonian

- ⚫ dry gin
- ⚫ Lillet
- 2 dashes crème de noyaux
- 2 dashes orange bitters

*Stir over ice. Strain into a cocktail glass and squeeze orange peel over.*

## Olivette

- ⚫⚫⚫ dry gin
- ⚫ pastis
- 2 dashes orange bitters
- 2 dashes sugar syrup

*Shake over ice. Strain into cocktail glasses and add a cocktail olive.*

## One Exciting Night

- ⚫ dry gin
- ⚫ dry vermouth
- ⚫ sweet vermouth
- ⚫ orange juice

*Dip cocktail glass first in orange juice and then in sugar to frost rim. Shake ingredients over ice. Strain into the prepared glass.*

## Opera

- ⚫ dry gin
- 4 dashes Dubonnet
- 4 dashes maraschino

*Stir over ice. Strain into a cocktail glass and squeeze orange peel over.*

## Orange Bloom

- ⚫⚫ dry gin
- ⚫ Cointreau
- ⚫ sweet vermouth

*Shake over ice. Strain into a cocktail glass and add a cocktail cherry.*

## Orange Blossom

- ⚫ dry gin
- ⚫ orange juice

*Shake over ice. Strain into a cocktail glass.*

## Orange Fizz

- ✗✗ dry gin
- ✗ Cointreau
- ✗ lemon juice
- ✗ orange juice
- teaspoon sugar
- chilled sparkling water

*Shake all but sparkling water over ice. Strain into tall, ice-filled glasses and top with sparkling water. Add orange slices.*

## Orange Martini

- ✗✗✗✗ dry gin
- ✗✗ dry vermouth
- ✗ sweet vermouth
- 2 dashes orange bitters
- peel of 1 orange

*Put all the ingredients except the orange bitters in a shaker and leave for at least 2 hours. Add ice and bitters and shake. Strain into cocktail glasses.*

## Orange Oasis

- ✗✗ dry gin
- ✗ cherry brandy
- ✗✗✗ orange juice
- chilled dry ginger ale

*Shake spirits and juice over ice. Strain into tall, ice-filled glasses and top with ginger ale.*

## Orient Express

- ✗ dry gin
- ✗ bourbon
- ✗ brandy

*Stir over ice. Strain into a cocktail glass.*

## Pall Mall

- ✗ dry gin
- ✗ dry vermouth
- ✗ sweet vermouth
- 4 dashes white crème de menthe
- dash orange bitters

*Stir over ice. Strain into a cocktail glass.*

## Palm Beach

- ⁙ dry gin
- ⁙ rum
- ⁙ pineapple

*Shake over ice. Strain into a cocktail glass.*

## Paradise

- ⁙ ⁙ dry gin
- ⁙ apricot brandy
- ⁙ orange juice

dash lemon juice

*Shake over ice. Strain into a cocktail glass.*

## Paris

- ⁙ dry gin
- ⁙ crème de cassis
- ⁙ dry vermouth

*Stir over ice. Strain into a cocktail glass.*

## Peggy

- ⁙ dry gin
- ⁙ dry vermouth

dash Dubonnet

dash pastis

*Stir over ice. Strain into a cocktail glass.*

## Pegu Club

- ⁙ dry gin
- ⁙ curaçao

4 dashes fresh lime juice

dash Angostura bitters

dash orange bitters

*Shake over ice. Strain into a cocktail glass.*

## Perfect

- ⁙ dry gin
- ⁙ dry vermouth
- ⁙ sweet vermouth

*Shake over ice. Strain into a cocktail glass.*

## Perfect Lady

- ▌▌ dry gin
- ▌ peach brandy
- ▌ lemon juice
- teaspoon egg white

*Shake over ice. Strain into a cocktail glass.*

## Peter Pan

- ▌ dry gin
- ▌ dry vermouth
- ▌ peach brandy
- ▌ orange juice

*Shake over ice. Strain into a cocktail glass.*

## Peto

- ▌▌ dry gin
- ▌ dry vermouth
- ▌ sweet vermouth
- ▌ orange juice
- 2 dashes maraschino

*Shake over ice. Strain into cocktail glasses.*

## Piccad

- ▌ dry gin
- ▌ Capéritif
- 2 dashes Angostura

*Stir over ice. Strain into a cocktail glass and add lemon slice.*

## Piccadilly

- ▌▌ dry gin
- ▌ dry vermouth
- dash grenadine
- dash pastis

*Stir over ice. Strain into a cocktail glass.*

## Pink Baby

- ▌▌ dry gin
- ▌ grenadine
- ▌ lemon syrup
- 1 egg white

*Shake over ice. Strain into cocktail glasses.*

## Pink Gin

⚱ dry gin

dash Angostura bitters

*Shake over ice. Strain into a cocktail glass.*

## Pink Lady

⚱⚱ dry gin

⚱ grenadine

1 egg white

*Shake over ice. Strain into a cocktail glass.*

## Pink Rose

⚱⚱⚱⚱ dry gin

⚱ grenadine

⚱ lemon juice

⚱ sweetened fresh cream

1 egg white

*Shake over ice. Strain into cocktail glasses.*

## Pinky

⚱⚱ dry gin

⚱ grenadine

1 egg white

*Shake over ice. Strain into cocktail glasses.*

## Playing Fields

⚱ dry gin

4 dashes crème de menthe

dash Angostura bitters

ginger beer

*Stir spirts and bitters in an ice-filled tumbler. Top with ginger beer. Add apple slice, maraschino cherry and mint sprig.*

## Plaza Sweet

⚱ dry gin

⚱ sweet vermouth

pinch caster sugar

*Stir over ice. Strain into cocktail glasses.*

---

When the clergyman's daughter drinks nothing but water, she's certain to finish on gin.

Rudyard Kipling

## Plymouth Cape

- ❚❚ Plymouth gin
- ❚ cranberry juice

*Shake over ice. Strain into a cocktail glass.*

## Poet's Dream

- ❚ dry gin
- ❚ dry vermouth
- dash Bénédictine
- dash orange bitters

*Shake over ice. Strain into cocktail glasses.*

## Pollyanna

- ❚❚ dry gin
- ❚ sweet vermouth
- 2 dashes grenadine
- slice of orange
- slice of pineapple

*Shake over ice. Strain into a cocktail glass.*

## Polo

- ❚ dry gin
- ❚ dry vermouth
- ❚ sweet vermouth
- 4 dashes lemon juice

*Shake over ice. Strain into a cocktail glass.*

## Poppy

- ❚❚ dry gin
- ❚ crème de cacao

*Stir over ice. Strain into a cocktail glass.*

## Prince Charles

- ❚❚ dry gin
- ❚ cherry brandy
- 2 dashes curaçao

*Stir over ice. Strain into a cocktail glass and squeeze orange peel over.*

The oldest distillery in England is that of Coates & Co at Plymouth, Devon. Founded in 1415, the building was formerly a Dominican monastery and then a lodging house. A number of the Pilgrim Fathers passed the night there before setting sail for America in the *Mayflower* (a vessel more accustomed to cargoes of wine) in 1620. Plymouth Gin has been distilled on the site since 1793.

## Princess Mary

- dry gin
- crème de cacao
- sweetened fresh cream

*Shake over ice. Strain into a cocktail glass.*

## Prince's Smile

- dry gin
- apple brandy
- apricot brandy

dash lemon juice

*Shake over ice. Strain into a cocktail glass.*

## Princeton

- dry gin
- port

2 dashes orange bitters

*Stir over ice. Strain into a cocktail glass and squeeze lemon peel over.*

## Pruneaux

- dry gin
- dry sherry
- orange juice
- prune syrup

*Shake over ice. Strain into ice-filled tumblers.*

## Puritan

- dry gin
- Lillet

2 dashes orange juice

dash apricot brandy

*Stir over ice. Strain into a cocktail glass.*

## Queen Elizabeth

- dry gin
- Cointreau
- lemon juice

dash pastis

*Shake over ice. Strain into a cocktail glass.*

## RAC

- ▮▮ dry gin
- ▮ dry vermouth
- ▮ sweet vermouth
- dash grenadine
- dash orange bitters

*Stir over ice. Strain into a cocktail glass. Add a maraschino cherry and squeeze orange peel over.*

## Racquet Club

- ▮ dry gin
- ▮ dry vermouth
- dash orange bitters

*Stir over ice. Strain into a cocktail glass.*

## Red Flag

- ▮ dry gin
- ▮ rum
- ▮ lemon juice
- ▮ pineapple juice
- dash grenadine

*Shake over ice. Strain into a cocktail glass.*

## Remsen Cooler

- ▮ dry gin
- 1 lemon
- soda water

*Peel the lemon to form a continuous spiral of rind. Suspend this in a tall tumbler and pack ice around it. Add gin and top with soda.*

## Renaissance

- ▮ dry gin
- ▮ dry sherry
- tablespoon fresh cream
- pinch nutmeg

*Shake gin, sherry and cream over ice. Strain into a cocktail glass and add nutmeg.*

## Resolute

- ▮▮ dry gin
- ▮ apricot brandy
- ▮ lemon juice

*Shake over ice. Strain into a cocktail glass.*

## Reverie

- ▮▮ dry gin
- ▮ Dubonnet
- ▮ Van der Hum

dash orange juice

*Shake over ice. Strain into a cocktail glass.*

## Richmond

- ▮▮ dry gin
- ▮ Lillet

*Stir over ice. Strain into a cocktail glass and squeeze lemon peel over.*

## Roc-a-Coe

- ▮ dry gin
- ▮ dry sherry

*Shake over ice. Strain into a cocktail glass and add a maraschino cherry.*

## Rolls-Royce 2

- ▮▮ dry gin
- ▮ dry vermouth
- ▮ sweet vermouth

dash Bénédictine

*Stir over ice. Strain into a cocktail glass.*

*This is a variation on an earlier (and less interesting) Rolls-Royce recipe. Devised by H. E. Bates for his 1958 novel* The Darling Buds of May.

## Rose

- ▮▮ dry gin
- ▮ cherry brandy
- ▮ dry vermouth

2 dashes lemon juice

*Stir over ice. Strain into cocktail glasses.*

---

The ▮ symbol in the recipes is a 'unit' to indicate proportions. A reasonable single measure to use in mixing is about an ounce – equivalent to 30 millilitres (ml). Quantities in the recipes given as dashes, spoonfuls etc., are based on one-ounce unit measures of the accompanying principal ingredients. A cocktail incorporating 2 to 3 measures of alcoholic ingredients makes a reasonably strong drink for one person. Cocktails with 4 or more measures are best made for two or more people.

### Rose de Chambertin

∎∎∎ dry gin

∎ crème de cassis

∎ fresh lime juice

teaspoon beaten egg white

teaspoon gomme syrup

*Prepare small wine glasses by dipping their rims in crème de cassis and then into caster sugar to frost. Shake the ingredients over ice and strain into the prepared glasses.*

### Roselyn

∎∎ dry gin

∎ dry vermouth

2 dashes grenadine

*Stir over ice. Strain into a cocktail glass and squeeze lemon peel over.*

### Royal 2

∎∎ dry gin

∎ lemon juice

1 egg

teaspoon sugar

*Shake over ice. Strain into a cocktail glass.*

### Royal Arrival

∎∎∎∎ dry gin

∎∎ lemon juice

∎ crème de noyaux

∎ kümmel

1 egg white

dash blue food colouring

*Shake over ice. Strain into cocktail glasses.*

### Royal Clover Club

∎ dry gin

4 dashes grenadine

4 dashes lemon juice

1 egg yoke

*Shake over ice. Strain into a cocktail glass.*

### Royal Fizz

∎∎ dry gin

∎ lemon juice

1 egg

teaspoon sugar

chilled soda water

*Shake all but soda over ice. Strain into ice-filled tumblers and top with soda. Add orange slice.*

## St Mark

∎∎ dry gin

∎∎ dry vermouth

∎ cherry brandy

∎ redcurrant syrup

*Stir over ice. Strain into cocktail glasses.*

## Salome

∎ dry gin

∎ dry vermouth

∎ Dubonnet

*Stir over ice. Strain into a cocktail glass.*

## Salty Dog

∎ dry gin

∎∎ grapefruit juice

salt

*Prepare a cocktail glass by dipping the rim in fruit juice and then in salt to encrust. Shake gin and juice over ice and strain.*

## Salutation

∎∎ dry gin

∎ Bénédictine

dash cherry brandy

*Stir over ice. Strain into a cocktail glass and add a maraschino cherry.*

## Sand Martin

∎∎ dry gin

∎∎ sweet vermouth

∎ green Chartreuse

*Stir over ice. Strain into cocktail glasses.*

## San Sebastian

∎∎∎ dry gin

∎ white rum

∎ Cointreau

∎ grapefruit juice

∎ fresh lime juice

*Shake over ice. Strain into cocktail glasses.*

---

Dr William Spooner, the Oxford professor and divine whose 'spoonerisms' made his philosophy lectures a legend, was elected to the office of warden of New College in 1903. Proposing the royal toast at the college dinner, he raised his glass in solemn devotion to 'the queer old dean'.

## Satan's Whiskers

∎∎ dry gin

∎∎ dry vermouth

∎∎ orange juice

∎ Grand Marnier

dash orange bitters

*Shake over ice. Strain into cocktail glasses.*

## Self-Starter

∎∎ dry gin

∎ Lillet

teaspoon apricot brandy

dash pastis

*Stir over ice. Strain into a cocktail glass.*

## Sensation

∎∎∎ dry gin

∎ lemon juice

3 dashes maraschino

3 sprigs fresh mint

*Shake over ice. Strain into a cocktail glass.*

## Seventh Heaven

∎ dry gin

∎ Capéritif

2 dashes maraschino

dash Angostura bitters

*Stir over ice. Strain into a cocktail glass and add a maraschino cherry.*

## Shady Grove

∎∎ dry gin

∎ lemon juice

teaspoon sugar

chilled ginger beer

*Pour gin, lemon and sugar into a tall ice-filled glass and top with ginger beer.*

## Silk Stocking

∎∎∎ dry gin

∎ apple brandy

∎∎ orange juice

*Shake over ice. Strain into cocktail glasses.*

# Silver

- ⁙ dry gin
- ⁙ dry vermouth
- 2 dashes maraschino
- 2 dashes orange bitters

*Stir over ice. Strain into a cocktail glass.*

# Silver Bells

- ⁙ dry gin
- ⁙ rum
- ⁙ lemon juice
- 2 dashes crème de noyaux

*Shake over ice. Strain into a cocktail glass.*

# Silver Bullet

- ⁙⁙ dry gin
- ⁙ kümmel
- ⁙ lemon juice

*Shake over ice. Strain into a cocktail glass.*

# Silver King

- ⁙⁙ dry gin
- ⁙ lemon juice
- 2 dashes orange bitters
- teaspoon sugar
- 1 egg white

*Shake over ice. Strain into a cocktail glass.*

---

An early recorded event in the history of mixed drinks is dated October 25th, 1599. On this occasion, Admiral of the Fleet Sir Edward Kennel invited six thousand officers and ratings from among his ships' crews to share a huge concoction served from a marble basin the size of a small swimming pool.

Into the mix went eighty barrels of brandy, a huge cask of malaga and a quantity of water, plus the juice of several thousand lemons and limes, half a ton of sugar and a sack of nutmeg.

The admiral had a canopy erected over the great vat to stop the rain diluting it. A young steward, bobbing on the brew in a rosewood boat, filled the thirsty guests' cups with a long-handled ladle. The servers were obliged to change watches every fifteen minutes, lest they became overwhelmed by the intoxicating fumes arising from the lowering swell.                                    *Spyglass*

## Silver Jubilee

- ▮▮ dry gin
- ▮▮ banana liqueur
- ▮ fresh cream

*Shake over ice. Strain into cocktail glasses.*

## Silver Streak

- ▮ dry gin
- ▮ kümmel

*Stir over ice. Strain into a cocktail glass.*

## Singapore Sling 2

- ▮▮ dry gin
- ▮ cherry brandy
- ▮ lemon juice
- teaspoon grenadine
- chilled soda water

*Shake over ice. Strain into ice-filled tall glasses and top with soda.*

*Another version of the Singapore Sling appears in the Fruit Brandies section.*

## Smile

- ▮ dry gin
- ▮ grenadine
- 3 dashes lemon juice

*Shake over ice. Strain into a cocktail glass.*

## Smiler

- ▮▮ dry gin
- ▮ dry vermouth
- ▮ sweet vermouth
- dash Angostura bitters
- dash orange bitters

*Stir over ice. Strain into a cocktail glass.*

## Snicker

- ▮▮ dry gin
- ▮ dry vermouth
- 2 dashes maraschino
- dash orange bitters
- teaspoon sugar
- 1 egg white

*Shake over ice. Strain into cocktail glasses.*

## Snowball 2

❚❚❚ dry gin

❚ Anisette

❚ crème de violette

❚ sweetened cream

*Shake over ice. Strain into cocktail glasses.*

*Another Snowball cocktail appears under Liqueurs & Apéritifs.*

## Snowflake

❚❚ dry gin

❚ lemon juice

❚ fresh cream

1 egg white

teaspoon grenadine

teaspoon sugar

chilled soda water

*Shake all but the soda over ice. Strain into tumblers and top with soda.*

## Snyder

❚❚ dry gin

❚ dry vermouth

teaspoon grapefruit juice

*Shake over ice. Strain into cocktail glasses.*

## Sorrento

❚❚ dry gin

❚ Galliano

❚ lemon juice

dash amaretto

*Shake over ice. Strain into cocktail glasses.*

## So-So

❚❚ dry gin

❚ sweet vermouth

❚ apple brandy

❚ grenadine

*Stir over ice. Strain into cocktail glasses.*

## Southern Gin

❚ dry gin

dash curaçao

dash orange bitters

*Stir over ice. Strain into a cocktail glass.*

## South Ken

- ▮ dry gin
- ▮ grapefruit juice
- ▮ pineapple juice
- dash Angostura bitters

*Shake over ice. Strain into a cocktail glass.*

## South Side

- ▮▮ dry gin
- ▮ lemon juice
- teaspoon sugar
- 2 mint sprigs

*Shake all but one mint sprig over ice. Strain into a cocktail glass and add remaining mint sprig.*

## Spencer

- ▮▮ dry gin
- ▮ apricot brandy
- dash Angostura bitters
- dash orange juice

*Shake over ice. Strain into a cocktail glass and add a maraschino cherry.*

## Sphinx

- ▮▮ dry gin
- ▮ dry vermouth
- ▮ sweet vermouth

*Stir over ice. Strain into cocktail glasses.*

## Spokane

- ▮▮ dry gin
- ▮ lemon juice
- 2 dashes sugar syrup

*Shake over ice. Strain into a cocktail glass.*

## Spring

- ▮▮▮ dry gin
- ▮ Bénédictine
- ▮ quinquina
- dash Angostura bitters

*Stir over ice. Strain into cocktail glasses.*

## Spring Feeling

- ▮▮ dry gin
- ▮ green Chartreuse
- ▮ lemon juice

*Shake over ice. Strain into cocktail glasses.*

## Stanley

- ▮▮ dry gin
- ▮▮ rum
- ▮ grenadine
- ▮ lemon juice

*Shake over ice. Strain into cocktail glasses.*

## Star

- ▮ dry gin
- ▮ apple brandy
- 4 dashes grapefruit
- dash dry vermouth
- dash sweet vermouth

*Shake over ice. Strain into a cocktail glass.*

## Star Daisy

- ▮▮ dry gin
- ▮▮ apple brandy
- ▮ crème de framboise
- ▮ lemon juice

*Shake over ice. Strain into cocktail glasses.*

## Straits Sling

- ▮ dry gin
- 4 dashes Bénédictine
- 4 dashes cherry brandy
- 4 dashes lemon juice
- dash Angostura bitters
- chilled soda water

*Shake over ice. Strain into a tall, ice-filled glass and top with soda.*

## Strawberry Slush

- ▮▮ dry gin
- ▮ lemon juice
- 8 small, fresh strawberries
- teaspoon sugar
- chilled soda water

*Mash strawberries with the lemon juice and sugar and divide between two tall tumblers. Add ice and gin. Top with soda and stir to mix.*

## Summertime

- ▮▮▮ dry gin
- ▮ lemon syrup

*Shake over ice. Strain into a cocktail glass.*

## Sunshine

▮▮ dry gin

▮ sweet vermouth

dash Angostura bitters

*Stir over ice. Strain into a cocktail glass.*

## Swan

▮ dry gin

▮ dry vermouth

dash Angostura bitters

dash lemon juice

*Shake over ice. Strain into a cocktail glass.*

## Sweet Patotie

▮▮ dry gin

▮ Cointreau

▮ orange juice

*Shake over ice. Strain into a cocktail glass.*

## Swizzles

▮ dry gin

▮ fresh lime juice

dash Angostura bitters

teaspoon sugar

*Shake over ice. Strain into a cocktail glass.*

## Tailspin

▮▮ dry gin

▮ sweet vermouth

▮ green Chartreuse

dash orange bitters

*Stir over ice. Strain into cocktail glasses.*

---

The ▮ symbol in the recipes is a 'unit' to indicate proportions. A reasonable single measure to use in mixing is about an ounce – equivalent to 30 millilitres (ml). Quantities in the recipes given as dashes, spoonfuls etc., are based on one-ounce unit measures of the accompanying principal ingredients. A cocktail incorporating 2 to 3 measures of alcoholic ingredients makes a reasonably strong drink for one person. Cocktails with 4 or more measures are best made for two or more people.

## Tango

- ■ ▮ dry gin
- ▮ dry vermouth
- ▮ sweet vermouth
- ▮ orange juice
- 2 dashes curaçao

*Shake over ice. Strain into cocktail glasses.*

## Tavern

- ■ ▮ dry gin
- ▮ dry vermouth
- ▮ sweet vermouth
- ▮ fresh lime juice
- dash pastis

*Shake over ice. Strain into cocktail glasses.*

## Third Degree

- ■ ▮ dry gin
- ▮ dry vermouth
- 2 dashes pastis

*Stir over ice. Strain into a cocktail glass.*

## This Is It

- ■ ▮ dry gin
- ▮ Cointreau
- ▮ lemon juice
- 1 egg white

*Shake over ice. Strain into cocktail glasses.*

## Three Stripes

- ■ ▮ dry gin
- ▮ dry vermouth
- ▮ orange juice

*Shake over ice. Strain into a cocktail glass.*

## Thunderclap

- ▮ dry gin
- ▮ Scotch whisky
- ▮ brandy

*Stir over ice. Strain into a cocktail glass.*

## Tipperary

- ▮▮ dry gin
- ▮▮ dry vermouth
- ▮ orange juice
- ▮ grenadine
- 2 sprigs mint

*Shake over ice. Strain into cocktail glasses.*

## Tom Collins

- ▮▮ dry gin
- ▮ lemon juice
- teaspoon sugar
- soda water

*Shake over ice. Strain into a tall, ice-filled glass and top with soda.*

## Transvaal

- ▮ dry gin
- ▮ Capéritif
- 2 dashes orange bitters

*Stir over ice. Strain into a cocktail glass.*

## Trinity

- ▮ dry gin
- ▮ dry vermouth
- ▮ sweet vermouth

*Stir over ice. Strain into a cocktail glass.*

## Turf

- ▮ dry gin
- ▮ dry vermouth
- 2 dashes pastis
- 4 dashes lemon juice

*Shake over ice. Strain into a cocktail glass.*

## Tuxedo

- ▮ dry gin
- ▮ dry vermouth
- 2 dashes orange bitters
- dash maraschino
- dash pastis

*Shake over ice. Strain into a cocktail glass.*

---

As I was the host at luncheon I . . . said to the interpreter that if it was the religion of His Majesty Ibn Saud to deprive himself of smoking and alcohol I must point out that my rule of life prescribed as an absolutely sacred rite the smoking of cigars and also the drinking of alcohol before, after and if need be during all meals and in the intervals between them.　Winston Churchill, *Triumph and Tragedy*

## Twin Six

- ▮▮▮ dry gin
- ▮ sweet vermouth
- 4 dashes orange juice
- dash grenadine
- 1 egg white

*Shake over ice. Strain into cocktail glasses.*

## Typhoon

- ▮▮ dry gin
- ▮ Anisette
- ▮▮ fresh lime juice
- chilled sparkling wine

*Shake spirits and lime over ice. Strain into tall ice-filled glasses and top with sparkling wine.*

## Ulanda

- ▮▮ dry gin
- ▮ Cointreau
- dash pastis

*Stir over ice. Strain into a cocktail glass.*

## Ultimate Beefeater Martini

- ▮ Beefeater gin
- dash dry vermouth

*Stir over ice. Strain into a cocktail glass and garnish with a sliver of fillet steak.*

*A New York variation on the eternal theme.*

## Union Jack (1)

- ▮▮▮ dry gin
- ▮ Crème Yvette

*Shake over ice. Strain into cocktail glasses.*

## Union Jack (2)

- ▮▮ dry gin
- ▮ sloe gin
- 3 dashes grenadine

*Stir over ice. Strain into a cocktail glass.*

## Van Dusen

- ▮▮ dry gin
- ▮ dry vermouth
- dash Grand Marnier

*Stir over ice. Strain into a cocktail glass.*

## Vespa

- dry gin
- 4 dashes vodka
- 2 dashes dry vermouth

*Shake over ice and strain into a cocktail glass.*

*Invention of Ian Fleming in Casino Royale for James Bond.*

## Victor's Special

- ❚❚ dry gin
- ❚ Cointreau
- ❚ lemon juice
- 1 egg white

*Shake over ice. Strain into a cocktail glass.*

## Vie en Rose

- ❚❚ dry gin
- ❚❚ kirsch
- ❚ lemon juice
- ❚ grenadine

*Stir over ice. Strain into cocktail glasses.*

## Virgin

- dry gin
- Forbidden Fruit
- white crème de menthe

*Stir over ice. Strain into a cocktail glass.*

## Wallis

- dry gin
- blue curaçao
- fresh lime juice
- sugar

*Encrust the rim of a cocktail glass by dipping it in fruit juice and then in sugar. Shake spirits and lime over ice and strain.*

---

In his twelve James Bond novels, Ian Fleming (1908–64) persistently specified that his hero's martinis should be shaken rather than stirred – a heretical practice, but one which Fleming always followed himself.

# Wall Street

- ▮▮ dry gin
- ▮ lemon juice
- teaspoon white crème de menthe
- chilled champagne

*Shake spirits and lemon juice over ice. Strain into a champagne glass and top with champagne.*

# Warday's

- ▮ dry gin
- ▮ apple brandy
- ▮ sweet vermouth
- 2 dashes Chartreuse

*Stir over ice. Strain into a cocktail glass.*

# Webster

- ▮▮ dry gin
- ▮ dry vermouth
- teaspoon apricot brandy
- teaspoon fresh lime juice

*Shake over ice. Strain into a cocktail glass.*

# Wedding Belle

- ▮▮ dry gin
- ▮▮ Dubonnet
- ▮ cherry brandy
- ▮ orange juice

*Shake over ice. Strain into cocktail glasses.*

# Weesuer Special

- ▮ dry gin
- ▮ dry vermouth
- ▮ sweet vermouth
- ▮ orange curaçao
- 4 dashes pastis

*Stir over ice. Strain into cocktail glasses.*

# Welcome Stranger

- ▮ dry gin
- ▮ brandy
- ▮ Swedish Punsch
- ▮ grenadine
- ▮ lemon juice
- ▮ orange juice
- dash Angostura bitters

*Shake over ice. Strain into cocktail glasses.*

## Wembley

▮▮ dry gin

▮ dry vermouth

2 dashes apple brandy

dash apricot brandy

*Stir over ice. Strain into a cocktail glass.*

## Westbrook

▮▮ dry gin

▮ sweet vermouth

4 dashes whisky

sprinkle of sugar

*Shake over ice. Strain into a cocktail glass.*

## Western Rose

▮▮ dry gin

▮ apricot brandy

▮ dry vermouth

dash lemon juice

*Shake over ice. Strain into a cocktail glass.*

## West Indian

▮ dry gin

teaspoon lemon juice

teaspoon sugar

4 dashes Angostura bitters

*Stir with an ice cube in a tumbler.*

## What the Dickens

▮ dry gin

teaspoon icing sugar

warm water

*Dissolve the sugar in the gin in a sturdy glass and top with warm water. Traditionally, the gin is poured from a milk jug, and the water from a teapot. A favourite with Mr and Mrs Bumble (in Oliver Twist).*

## What the Hell

▮ dry gin

▮ apricot brandy

▮ dry vermouth

dash lemon juice

*Stir over ice. Strain into a cocktail glass.*

## White Baby

- ▮▮ dry gin
- ▮ Cointreau
- ▮ lemon syrup

*Shake over ice. Strain into a cocktail glass.*

## White Cargo

- ▮ dry gin
- ▮ vanilla ice cream

*Shake, thinning as necessary with iced water.*

## White Knight

- ▮▮ dry gin
- 4 dashes Anisette
- dash orange bitters

*Stir over ice. Strain into a cocktail glass and squeeze lemon peel over.*

## White Lady

- ▮▮ dry gin
- ▮ Cointreau
- ▮ lemon juice

*Shake over ice. Strain into a cocktail glass.*

## White Lily

- ▮ dry gin
- ▮ rum
- ▮ Cointreau
- dash pastis

*Stir over ice. Strain into a cocktail glass.*

## White Plush

- 2 dashes dry gin
- ▮ milk
- dash maraschino

*Shake over ice. Strain into a cocktail glass.*

---

The ▮ symbol in the recipes is a 'unit' to indicate proportions. A reasonable single measure to use in mixing is about an ounce – equivalent to 30 millilitres (ml). Quantities in the recipes given as dashes, spoonfuls etc., are based on one-ounce unit measures of the accompanying principal ingredients. A cocktail incorporating 2 to 3 measures of alcoholic ingredients makes a reasonably strong drink for one person. Cocktails with 4 or more measures are best made for two or more people.

## White Rose

▮▮▮ dry gin

▮ maraschino

▮ orange juice

4 dashes lemon juice

*Shake over ice. Strain into cocktail glasses.*

## White Way

▮▮ dry gin

▮ white crème de menthe

*Stir over ice. Strain into cocktail glasses.*

## White Wings

▮▮ dry gin

▮ white crème de menthe

*Stir over ice. Strain into a cocktail glass.*

## Why Not

▮▮ dry gin

▮ apricot brandy

▮ dry vermouth

2 dashes lemon juice

*Shake over ice. Strain into cocktail glasses.*

## Will Rogers

▮▮ dry gin

▮ dry vermouth

▮ orange juice

4 dashes curaçao

*Shake over ice. Strain into a cocktail glass.*

## Windsor Rose

▮▮▮ dry gin

▮▮ Dubonnet

▮ Campari

dash crème de noyaux

*Stir over ice. Strain into cocktail glasses.*

## Xanthia

▮ dry gin

▮ cherry brandy

▮ yellow Chartreuse

*Stir over ice. Strain into a cocktail glass.*

## Yale

▌ dry gin

3 dashes orange bitters

dash Angostura bitters

soda water

*Stir gin and bitters over ice. Strain into a cocktail glass. Add a little soda and squeeze lemon peel over.*

## Yankee Prince

▌▌▌ dry gin

▌ Grand Marnier

▌ orange juice

*Shake over ice. Strain into cocktail glasses.*

## Yarlington

▌ dry gin

▌ Cointreau

▌ pineapple juice

*Shake over ice. Strain into a cocktail glass.*

## Yellow Daisy

▌▌ dry gin

▌▌ dry vermouth

▌ Grand Marnier

dash pastis

*Stir over ice. Strain into cocktail glasses.*

## Yellow Rattler

▌ dry gin

▌ dry vermouth

▌ sweet vermouth

▌ orange juice

dash Angostura bitters

*Shake over ice. Strain into a cocktail glass and add a cocktail onion.*

# LIQUEURS & APÉRITIFS

This is something of a catch-all section. Liqueurs are taken to be spirit-based flavoured drinks – as distinct from fruit brandies, which are distilled at least partially from the fruits whose names they bear. Apéritifs are those countless generic and branded drinks which defy other description – with the notable exception of vermouth, which has a section to itself. If some of the branded or generic ingredients included here seem unfamiliar, see the glossary for brief descriptions.

## Absolute Peach

- peach schnapps
- Absolut vodka

*Stir over ice. Strain into a shot glass.*

## After Dinner

- Cointreau
- apricot brandy
- fresh lime juice

*Shake over ice. Strain into a cocktail glass.*

## After Dinner 2

- prunelle liqueur
- cherry brandy
- lemon juice

*Shake over ice. Strain into a cocktail glass.*

## After One

- Campari
- dry gin
- sweet vermouth
- Galliano

*Stir over ice. Strain into cocktail glasses.*

## After Supper

- Cointreau
- apricot brandy
- lemon juice

*Shake over ice. Strain into a cocktail glass.*

## Agadir

- Tia Maria
- orange juice
- chilled sparkling wine

*Stir liqueur and juice in a tall glass filled with ice. Top with sparkling wine.*

## Alabama Slammer

- Southern Comfort
- amaretto
- teaspoon sloe gin
- dash lemon juice

*Stir over ice. Strain into a shot glass.*

## Albertine

- kirsch
- green Chartreuse
- Cointreau
- dash maraschino

*Stir over ice. Strain into a cocktail glass.*

## Amaretto Coffee

- amaretto
- cup of hot, black coffee
- whipped fresh cream

*Add amaretto to coffee. Float cream on top.*

## Amaretto Cream

- amaretto
- fresh cream

*Shake over ice. Strain into a cocktail glass.*

## Amaretto Rose

- amaretto
- teaspoon Rose's Lime Juice cordial
- soda water

*Pour amaretto and lime into an ice-filled tall glass. Top with soda.*

## Amaretto Stinger

- ❚❚ amaretto
- ❚ crème de menthe

*Shake over ice. Strain into a cocktail glass.*

## Americano

- ❚ Campari
- ❚ sweet vermouth
- soda water

*Pour over ice in a tall glass. Top with soda, stir and add an orange slice.*

## Angel's Kiss

- ❚ crème de cacao
- ❚ sloe gin
- ❚ brandy
- ❚ single cream

*Chill all the ingredients in the refrigerator. To make two drinks, pour half of each measure into a pair of shot glasses, in the order given, keeping your hand steady to avoid mixing the ingredients.*

## Banana

- ❚ banana liqueur
- ❚ rum
- ❚ fresh cream
- 4 dashes orange juice
- dash Angostura bitters
- dash grenadine

*Shake all ingredients except grenadine over ice. Strain into an ice-filled tumbler and add grenadine.*

## Banana Slip

- ❚ chilled banana liqueur
- ❚ chilled Baileys Irish Cream

*Chill the liqueurs in the refrigerator in advance. Pour each in turn into a liqueur or shot glass, so that the two liqueurs remain separate.*

## Banshee

- ❚❚ banana liqueur
- ❚ crème de cacao
- ❚ fresh cream

*Shake over ice. Strain into cocktail glasses.*

## Bazooka

- ✹✹✹ Green Chartreuse
- ✹ brandy
- ✹ cherry brandy
- ✹ dry gin

*Stir over ice. Strain into cocktail glasses and add a maraschino cherry to each.*

## B-52

- ✹ crème de cacao
- ✹ Baileys Irish Cream
- ✹ Grand Marnier

*Chill the ingredients in the refrigerator in advance. Pour each in turn into a shot glass. Keep your hand steady to avoid mixing the ingredients.*

## Bill Gibb

- ✹ Mandarine Napoléon
- ✹ dry gin
- ✹✹✹✹ freshly squeezed orange juice

dash Angostura

*Shake over ice. Strain into an ice-filled tall tumber.*

*Commemorates the late London couturier, for whom the drink was devised by Charles, barman in the former Grill Room bar at London's Hyde Park Hotel.*

---

The ✹ symbol in the recipes is a 'unit' to indicate proportions. A reasonable single measure to use in mixing is about an ounce – equivalent to 30 millilitres (ml). Quantities in the recipes given as dashes, spoonfuls etc., are based on one-ounce unit measures of the accompanying principal ingredients. A cocktail incorporating 2 to 3 measures of alcoholic ingredients makes a reasonably strong drink for one person. Cocktails with 4 or more measures are best made for two or more people.

## Black Maria

- ∎ Tia Maria
- ∎ rum
- ∎ black coffee, chilled
- teaspoon sugar

*Stir over ice in a brandy glass.*

## Blackthorn

- ∎ sloe gin
- ∎ sweet vermouth

*Stir over ice. Strain into a cocktail glass.*

## Blanche

- ∎ Cointreau
- ∎ white curaçao
- ∎ Anisette

*Stir over ice. Strain into a cocktail glass.*

## Block and Tackle

- ∎∎ Cointreau
- ∎∎ brandy
- ∎ apple brandy
- ∎ pastis

*Stir over ice. Strain into cocktail glasses.*

## Boniface

- ∎∎ Cointreau
- ∎∎ orange juice
- 2 teaspoons sugar
- 2 egg yolks
- chilled sparkling wine

*Shake all but the sparkling wine over ice. Strain into wine glasses and top with sparkling wine.*

## Broadway Smile

- ∎ chilled Cointreau
- ∎ chilled crème de cassis
- ∎ chilled Swedish Punsch

*Gently pour each liqueur into a small tumbler. They should not mix.*

## Brown Cow

- ∎ Kahlúa
- ∎∎∎ fresh milk

*Shake over ice. Strain into an ice-filled tumbler.*

## Bushwhacker

- ▮ Baileys Irish Cream
- ▮ rum
- ▮ Tia Maria
- ▮ amaretto
- ▮▮▮▮ fresh cream

*Shake over ice. Strain into ice-filled tumblers.*

## Byculla

- ▮ ginger wine
- ▮ curaçao
- ▮ port
- ▮ sherry

*Stir over ice. Strain into cocktail glasses.*

## Byrrh

- ▮ Byrrh
- ▮ rye whiskey
- ▮ dry vermouth

*Stir over ice. Strain into a cocktail glass.*

## Byrrh Cassis

- ▮▮ Byrrh
- ▮ crème de cassis
- soda water

*Mix the lqueurs in an ice-filled glass. Top with soda.*

## Café Kirsch

- ▮ kirsch
- ▮▮ cold black coffee
- teaspoon sugar
- 1 egg white

*Shake over ice. Strain into cocktail glasses.*

## Calm Sea

- ▮ Strega
- ▮ rum
- ▮ crème de cassis
- 4 dashes lemon juice
- 1 egg white

*Shake over ice. Strain into cocktail glasses.*

---

No animal ever invented anything so bad as drunkenness – or so good as drink.                                    G. K. Chesterton

# Canadian

- ⠿ curaçao
- ⠇ rum
- ⠇ lemon juice
- teaspoon caster sugar

*Shake over ice. Strain into cocktail glasses.*

# Cara Sposa

- ⠇ Tia Maria
- ⠇ Cointreau
- ⠇ fresh cream

*Shake over ice. Strain into a cocktail glass.*

# Charleston

- ⠇ curaçao
- ⠇ kirsch
- ⠇ dry gin
- ⠇ dry vermouth
- ⠇ sweet vermouth
- ⠇ maraschino

*Stir over ice. Strain into cocktail glasses.*

# Charlie Chaplin

- ⠇ sloe gin
- ⠇ apricot brandy
- ⠇ lemon juice

*Shake over ice. Strain into a shot glass.*

# Chocolate

- ⠇ yellow Chartreuse
- ⠇ maraschino
- 1 teaspoon powdered chocolate
- 1 egg

*Shake over ice. Strain into cocktail glasses.*

# Corsican Breeze

- ⠇ Mandarine Napoléon
- ⠿ chilled bitter lemon
- ⠿ chilled orange juice

*Combine in a tall glass and add ice cubes. Add a mint sprig.*

## Crème de Menthe Frappé

■■ green crème de menthe

*Fill a small brandy glass with crushed ice and pour liqueur over. Serve with two short straws.*

## Cresta Run

■■ kirsch

■ dry vermouth

teaspoon crème de noyaux

*Stir over ice. Strain into a cocktail glass and add orange peel.*

## Curaçao

■ kirsch

■ orange juice

4 dashes brandy

4 dashes gin

dash orange bitters

*Shake over ice. Strain into a cocktail glass.*

## Diabola

■■ Dubonnet

■ dry gin

2 dashes Orgeat syrup

*Stir over ice. Strain into a cocktail glass.*

## Diana

■■■ white crème de menthe

■ brandy

*Pour into a small wine glass filled with crushed ice.*

## Doctor

■■ Swedish Punsch

■ lemon juice

*Shake over ice. Strain into a cocktail glass.*

---

In the greeny-greeny gloom
Sits this drunkard in his room
Glug-glugging from his schnapps
Till he's ready to collapse
                    Bertolt Brecht, translated by Edward Baxter

## Dodge Special

- ⚌ Cointreau
- ⚌ dry gin
- dash grape juice

*Shake over ice. Strain into a cocktail glass.*

## Dubonnet Cocktail

- ⚌⚌ Dubonnet
- ⚌ dry gin

*Stir over ice. Strain into a cocktail glass.*

## Dubonnet Fizz

- ⚌⚌ Dubonnet
- ⚌ cherry brandy
- ⚌ orange juice
- 4 dashes lemon juice
- soda water

*Shake all but the soda over ice. Strain into tall ice-filled glasses and top with soda.*

## Duke

- ⚌ Cointreau
- ⚌ equal mix of lemon and orange juice
- 2 dashes maraschino
- 1 egg white
- sparkling wine

*Shake all but the sparkling wine over ice. Strain into wine glasses and top with sparkling wine.*

## Fanny Hill

- ⚌ Campari
- ⚌ Cointreau
- ⚌ brandy
- chilled sparkling wine

*Stir spirits over ice. Strain into champagne glasses and top with sparkling wine.*

## Fifth Avenue

- ⚌ chilled crème de cacao
- ⚌ chilled apricot brandy
- tablespoon chilled fresh cream

*Pour the ingredients into a liqueur glass in turn so that each forms a separate layer.*

## Five-Fifteen

- ⚫ curaçao
- ⚫ dry vermouth
- ⚫ sweetened fresh cream

*Shake over ice. Strain into a cocktail glass.*

## Fluffy Navel

- ⚫ peach schnapps
- ⚫ fresh orange juice

*Shake over ice. Strain into a cocktail glass.*

*Also known as Fuzzy Navel.*

## Frank Sullivan

- ⚫ Cointreau
- ⚫ brandy
- ⚫ Lillet
- ⚫ lemon juice

*Shake over ice. Strain into a cocktail glass.*

## Freedom Fighter

- ⚫⚫⚫ sloe gin
- ⚫ Crème Yvette
- ⚫ lemon juice
- 1 egg white

*Shake over ice. Strain into small wine glasses.*

## Genoa

- ⚫⚫ grappa
- ⚫⚫ dry gin
- ⚫ Sambuca
- ⚫ dry vermouth

*Stir over ice. Strain into cocktail glasses.*

## Gloom Chaser

- ⚫ curaçao
- ⚫ Grand Marnier
- ⚫ grenadine
- ⚫ lemon juice

*Shake over ice. Strain into cocktail glasses.*

## Golden Cadillac

- Cointreau
- Galliano
- fresh cream

*Shake over ice. Strain into a cocktail glass.*

## Golden Dream

- Galliano
- Cointreau
- fresh cream

dash orange bitters

*Shake over ice. Strain into cocktail glasses.*

## Golden Nipple

- Galliano
- Baileys Irish Cream

*Shake over ice. Strain into a liqueur glass.*

## Golden Slipper

- Eau de Vie de Danzig
- yellow Chartreuse

1 egg yolk

*Shake over ice. Strain into a cocktail glass.*

## Grand Slam

- Swedish Punsch
- dry vermouth
- sweet vermouth

*Stir over ice. Strain into cocktail glasses.*

## Grappa-Strega

- grappa
- Strega
- equal mix lemon and orange juice

*Shake over ice. Strain into a cocktail glass.*

Baileys Irish Cream was launched in 1974 and has already become the world's leading liqueur brand. The 40 million gallons of milk used to make Baileys each year now account for a third of Ireland's total liquid-milk production. One per cent of all the Republic's export earnings is accounted for by Baileys.

## Grasshopper

- white crème de menthe
- green crème de menthe
- fresh cream

*Shake over ice. Strain into a cocktail glass.*

## Grasshopper Surprise

- crème de cacao
- crème de menthe
- fresh cream

*Shake over ice. Strain into a cocktail glass*

## Helen Twelvetrees

- Southern Comfort

2 dashes blackberry concentrate

dry ginger ale

*Stir liqueur and blackberry in an ice-filled tall glass. Top with ginger ale.*

## Hell

- crème de menthe
- cognac

cayenne pepper

*Stir the spirits over ice. Strain into a cocktail glass and add a pinch of the cayenne.*

## Hesitation

- Swedish Punsch
- rye whiskey

dash lemon juice

*Shake over ice. Strain into cocktail glasses.*

## Honeymoon

- Bénédictine
- apple brandy
- lemon juice

3 dashes curaçao

*Shake over ice. Strain into cocktail glasses.*

# Honolulu

- Bénédictine
- dry gin
- maraschino

*Stir over ice. Strain into a cocktail glass.*

# Hoopla

- Cointreau
- brandy
- Lillet
- lemon juice

*Shake over ice. Strain into a cocktail glass.*

# Hundred Per Cent

- ⫶⫶ Swedish Punsch

teaspoon lemon juice

teaspoon orange juice

2 dashes grenadine

*Shake over ice. Strain into a cocktail glass.*

# Irish Charlie

- Baileys Irish Cream
- white crème de menthe

*Stir over ice. Strain into a cocktail glass.*

# Irish Mint

- Baileys Irish Cream
- white crème de menthe

*Stir over ice. Strain into a shot glass.*

# Italiano

- amaretto
- brandy

chilled pineapple juice

*Pour spirits into an ice-filled tall glass. Top with pineapple juice. Stir to mix.*

# Jewel

- green Chartreuse
- dry gin
- sweet vermouth

2 dashes orange bitters

*Stir over ice. Strain into a cocktail glass and add a maraschino cherry.*

# Johnnie Mack

- ⫶⫶ sloe gin
- orange curaçao

3 dashes pastis

*Stir over ice. Strain into a cocktail glass.*

## Kahlúa Cocktail

**❚** Kahlúa

dash crème de noyaux

teaspoon fresh cream

*Stir liqueurs in an ice-filled tumbler. Float cream on top.*

## Kamikaze

**❚** Cointreau

**❚** vodka

**❚** Rose's Lime Juice cordial

*Shake over ice. Strain into a shot glass.*

## L'Aiglon

**❚** Mandarine Napoléon

chilled champagne

*Pour Mandarine into a champagne flûte glass and top with champagne.*

## Lillet Cocktail

**❚❚** Lillet

**❚** dry gin

*Stir over ice. Strain into a cocktail glass and add a lemon peel twist.*

## Long Shot

**❚❚❚** blackberry liqueur

**❚** orange juice

4 dashes lemon juice

dash orange bitters

chilled dry ginger ale

*Pour the ingredients, in the above sequence, into an ice-filled tall glass, topping up with the ginger ale. Stir.*

---

The ❚ symbol in the recipes is a 'unit' to indicate proportions. A reasonable single measure to use in mixing is about an ounce – equivalent to 30 millilitres (ml). Quantities in the recipes given as dashes, spoonfuls etc., are based on one-ounce unit measures of the accompanying principal ingredients. A cocktail incorporating 2 to 3 measures of alcoholic ingredients makes a reasonably strong drink for one person. Cocktails with 4 or more measures are best made for two or more people.

## Love

- ▮▮ sloe gin
- 2 dashes lemon juice
- 2 dashes lemon juice
- 1 egg white

*Shake over ice. Strain into a cocktail glass.*

## Lulu

- ▮▮ Cointreau
- ▮ melon juice
- ▮ orange juice

*Shake over ice. Strain into a cocktail glass.*

## Maiden's Prayer

- ▮ Cointreau
- ▮ dry gin
- teaspoon lemon juice
- teaspoon orange juice

*Shake over ice. Strain into a cocktail glass.*

## Mandarine Sour

- ▮ Mandarine Napoléon
- ▮ lemon juice
- dash triple sec

*Stir into crushed ice in a cocktail glass.*

## Manyann

- ▮▮ Capéritif
- ▮▮ dry gin
- ▮ lemon juice
- 2 dashes curaçao

*Shake over ice. Strain into cocktail glasses.*

## Margarita Impériale

- ▮ Mandarine Napoléon
- ▮ tequila
- ▮ lemon juice
- dash curaçao

*Shake over ice. Strain into a cocktail glass.*

---

Shooters and slammers are cocktails served in small 'shot' glasses for drinking in one gulp. Liqueur-based shooters are commonly prepared by gently pouring each ingredient in turn into the glass so they do not mix, but form colourful layers.

## McClelland

■■ sloe gin

■ curaçao

dash pastis

*Stir over ice. Strain into a cocktail glass.*

## Melba

■■ Swedish Punsch

■■ rum

4 dashes lemon juices

dash grenadine

dash pastis

*Shake over ice. Strain into cocktail glasses.*

## Melon Balls

■ melon liqueur

■ vodka

■ pineapple juice

*Shake over ice. Strain into a cocktail glass.*

## Mocha Mint

■ crème de cacao

■ crème de menthe

■ Tia Maria

*Stir over ice. Strain into a cocktail glass.*

## Mona Lisa

■■■ crème de cacao

■ dry vermouth

lemon juice

sugar

*Prepare cocktail glasses by dipping rims in lemon juice, then in sugar to encrust. Stir liqueur and vermouth over ice and strain.*

## Moulin Rouge 2

■■ sloe gin

■ sweet vermouth

dash Angostura bitters

*Stir over ice. Strain into cocktail glasses.*

*There is another Moulin Rouge recipe in the Fruit Brandies section.*

## Napobitter

- Mandarine Napoléon
- chilled bitter lemon

*Pour liqueur into a tall, ice-filled glass. Top with bitter lemon.*

## Napoleon's Redemption

- Mandarine Napoléon
- vodka
- chilled tonic water

*Pour spirits over ice in a tall glass. Top with tonic and add orange slice.*

## Negroni

- Campari
- dry gin
- sweet vermouth

*Stir over ice. Strain into a cocktail glass.*

*The drink was devised by Count Negroni at the Bar Giacosa in Florence.*

## Nutty Professor

- Baileys Irish Cream
- crème de noyaux
- Grand Marnier

*Stir over ice. Strain into a cocktail glass.*

## Odd McIntyre

- Cointreau
- Lillet
- brandy
- lemon juice

*Shake over ice. Strain into a cocktail glass.*

## Oh, Henry!

- Bénédictine
- whisky
- dry ginger ale

*Stir over ice. Strain into a cocktail glass.*

## Old Pal

- Campari
- dry vermouth
- rye whiskey

*Stir over ice. Strain into a cocktail glass.*

## Old Trout

- ▮ Campari
- ▮▮ fresh orange juice

chilled sparkling water

*Shake Campari and orange over ice. Strain into an ice-filled tall glass and top with sparkling water. Add orange slice.*

## Ostend Fizz

- ▮ crème de cassis
- ▮ kirsch
- ▮ lemon juice

chilled sparkling water

*Shake liqueurs and lemon over ice. Strain into an ice-filled tumbler and top with sparkling water.*

## Parisian

- ▮ crème de cassis
- ▮ dry gin
- ▮ dry vermouth

*Stir over ice. Strain into a cocktail glass.*

## Parisian Blonde

- ▮ curaçao
- ▮ rum
- ▮ sweetened fresh cream

*Shake over ice. Strain into a cocktail glass.*

## Phoebe Snow

- ▮ Dubonnet
- ▮ brandy

dash pastis

*Shake over ice. Strain into a small wine glass filled with crushed ice.*

Royal pretender Bonnie Prince Charlie is said to have given the recipe for Drambuie to a faithful supporter, Mackinnon of Strathaird, who helped him escape to France after the abortive rebellion of 1745. The prince's grateful token remained a secret of the Mackinnons until 1906 when the family went into commercial production. The name Drambuie is Gaelic for the 'drink that satisfies'.

## Pimm's Cooler

- ∷ Pimm's No. 1
- ∷ fresh lime juice
- ∶ fresh lemon juice
- dash Cointreau
- pinch caster sugar

*Shake over ice. Strain into a tall ice-filled glass and top with soda. Add lime slice.*

## Ping Pong

- ∷ Crème Yvette
- ∷ sloe gin
- ∶ lemon juice

*Shake over ice. Strain into cocktail glasses.*

## Pink Squirrel

- ∶ crème de noyaux
- ∶ crème de cacao
- ∶ fresh cream

*Shake over ice. Strain into a cocktail glass.*

## Plantation Punch

- ∶ Southern Comfort
- ∶ rum
- ∶ lemon juice
- teaspoon sugar
- chilled sparkling water

*Shake all but the sparkling water over ice. Strain into ice-filled tumblers and top with sparkling water. Add lemon slices and maraschino cherries.*

## Platinum Blonde

- ∶ Cointreau
- ∶ rum
- ∶ fresh cream

*Shake over ice. Strain into a cocktail glass.*

---

Pimm's is named after London fish restaurateur James Pimm, who devised the drink for his customers in the nineteenth century. Pimm's is gin compounded with a secret mixture of liqueurs, herbs and essences. The makers recommend a 'Pimms' should be made in a half-pint tankard with 1½ oz Pimm's, ice cubes, a twist of lemon peel and a slice of cucumber rind. Top up with chilled lemonade or dry ginger ale.

## Poop Deck

- ▮▮ blackberry liqueur
- ▮ brandy
- ▮ port

*Stir over ice. Strain into cocktail glasses.*

## Princess Mary

- ▮ crème de cacao
- ▮ dry gin
- ▮ sweetened fresh cream

*Shake over ice. Strain into a cocktail glass.*

## Queen of Denmark

- ▮▮ Cherry Heering
- teaspoon fresh cream

*Pour Cherry Heering into a small wine glass. Float cream on top.*

## Raffles Knockout

- ▮ Cointreau
- ▮ kirsch
- dash lemon juice

*Shake over ice. Strain into a cocktail glass and add a cocktail cherry.*

## Rainbow

- ▮ crème de cacao
- ▮ crème de violette
- ▮ green Chartreuse
- ▮ yellow Chartreuse
- ▮ maraschino
- ▮ Bénédictine
- ▮ brandy

*The idea of this challenging cocktail is to pour each spirit into the glass very gently so it doesn't mix with the one below. The aim, ultimately, is to create a multi-coloured, striped whole. Choose a tall, narrow-bowled, stemmed glass (such as a small champagne flûte) and apply a steady hand.*

---

Chartreuse has been produced at the Carthusian monastery of La Grande Chartreuse (est. 1054) since 1764 to the same recipe, incorporating 130 different flavouring ingredients. Yellow Chartreuse is 40 per cent alcohol by volume, and the drier, spicier Green is very much stronger at 55 per cent.

## Rattlesnake

- ⦙ chilled Baileys Irish Cream
- ⦙ chilled crème de cacao
- ⦙ chilled Kahlúa

*Into a liqueur or shot glass, gently pour the ingredients in turn. They should form three separate layers.*

## Red Lion

- ⦙⦙ Grand Marnier
- ⦙ dry gin
- ⦙ lemon juice
- ⦙ orange juice

*Shake over ice. Strain into cocktail glasses.*

## Rocky Mountain

- ⦙ amaretto
- ⦙ Southern Comfort
- teaspoon fresh lime juice

*Shake over ice. Strain into a shot glass.*

## Royal Jamaican

- ⦙⦙⦙ Tia Maria
- ⦙ fresh cream

*Shake over ice. Strain into cocktail glasses.*

## Royal Wedding

- ⦙ kirsch
- ⦙ peach brandy
- ⦙⦙ orange juice

*Shake over ice. Strain into a cocktail glass*

## Roy Howard

- ⦙⦙ Lillet
- ⦙ brandy
- ⦙ orange juice
- 2 dashes grenadine

*Shake over ice. Strain into a cocktail glass.*

## Rusty Nail

- ⦙ Drambuie
- ⦙ Scotch whisky

*Stir over ice. Strain into a cocktail glass.*

## St Andrew's

- ▮ Drambuie
- ▮ Scotch whisky
- ▮ orange juice

*Shake over ice. Strain into a cocktail glass.*

## St Germain

- ▮▮ green Chartreuse
- ▮ grapefruit juice
- ▮ lemon juice
- 1 egg white

*Shake over ice. Strain into cocktail glasses.*

## Sambuca Shooter

- ▮ Sambuca
- tablespoon vodka
- tablespoon fresh cream

*Shake over ice. Strain into a shot glass.*

## Savoy Corpse Reviver

- ▮ Fernet Branca
- ▮ white crème de menthe
- ▮ brandy

*Stir over ice. Strain into a cocktail glass.*

## Scarlett O'Hara

- ▮▮ Southern Comfort
- ▮ cranberry juice
- dash lime juice

*Shake over ice. Strain into a cocktail glass.*

## Shriner

- ▮ sloe gin
- ▮ brandy
- dash Angostura bitters
- pinch of sugar

*Shake over ice. Strain into a cocktail glass.*

## Slippery Nipple

- ▮ Baileys Irish Cream
- teaspoon Sambuca

*Stir Baileys over ice to chill and pour into a liqueur glass. Float Sambuca on top.*

## Sloeberry

- ▮ sloe gin
- dash Angostura bitters
- dash orange bitters

*Stir over ice. Strain into a cocktail glass.*

## Sloe Gin Cocktail

- ❚❚ sloe gin
- ❚ dry vermouth
- ❚ sweet vermouth

*Stir over ice. Strain into a cocktail glass.*

## Sloe Measure

- ❚ sloe gin
- ❚ Lillet
- 2 dashes crème de noyaux
- 2 dashes orange bitters

*Stir over ice. Strain into a cocktail glass.*

## Sloe Vermouth

- ❚❚ sloe gin
- ❚❚ dry vermouth
- ❚ lemon juice

*Shake over ice. Strain into cocktail glasses.*

## Snowball

- ❚ advocaat
- chilled lemonade

*Pour advocaat into a stemmed glass and top with lemonade. Add an orange slice and a cocktail cherry.*

## Sombrero

- ❚❚ Tia Maria
- ❚ fresh cream

*Shake over ice. Strain into a cocktail glass.*

## Sony & Cher

- ❚ crème de cassis
- ❚ sake
- chilled sparkling wine

*Stir cassis and sake over ice. Strain into a flûte glass and top with sparkling wine.*

---

Advocaat has been made in the Netherlands for centuries and is the most widely exported of all Dutch liqueurs. Advocaat is made from a combination of fresh egg yolks, brandy, sugar and vanilla. Export brands are thinned for ease of pouring. Advocaats for domestic consumption are commonly thick enough to stand a spoon in.

## Southern Peach

- ⚏ Southern Comfort
- ⚏ peach brandy
- ⚏ fresh cream

  dash Angostura bitters

*Shake over ice. Strain into a cocktail glass and add a slice of fresh peach.*

## Spion Kop

- ⚏ Capéritif
- ⚏ dry vermouth

*Stir over ice. Strain into a cocktail glass.*

## Springbok

- ⚏ Lillet
- ⚏ Van der Hum
- ⚏ dry sherry

  2 dashes orange bitters

*Stir over ice. Strain into a cocktail glass.*

## Stars & Stripes

- ⚏ crème de cassis
- ⚏ green Chartreuse
- ⚏ maraschino

*For a colourfully striped cocktail, pour each ingredient in turn into a liqueur glass, being careful to avoid any mixing.*

## Strega Flip

- ⚏⚏ Strega
- ⚏⚏ brandy
- ⚏ orange juice

  4 dashes lemon juice

  1 egg

  teaspoon sugar

  pinch of nutmeg

*Shake all but the nutmeg over ice. Strain into cocktail glasses and add nutmeg over.*

## Sunrise

- crème violette
- Cointreau
- yellow Chartreuse
- grenadine

*For a striped cocktail, pour each ingredient in turn into a liqueur glass, being careful to avoid any mixing.*

## Suzie

- Suze
- dry gin

dash orange bitters

*Stir over ice. Strain into a cocktail glass.*

## Swazi Freeze

- Capéritif
- rye whiskey

dash peach brandy

*Stir over ice. Strain into a cocktail glass.*

## Three-Quarter Back

- curaçao
- yellow Chartreuse
- brandy

*For a striped cocktail, pour each ingredient in turn into a liqueur glass, being careful to avoid any mixing.*

## Titanic

- Mandarine Napoléon
- vodka

chilled sparkling water

*Shake spirits over ice. Strain into ice-filled tumbler and top with sparkling water.*

## Treble Chance

- Cointreau
- whisky
- dry vermouth

*Stir over ice. Strain into a cocktail glass.*

Suze, the distinctively gentian-flavoured and gold-coloured drink of France, is made by Pernod. It is said to divide opinion more than any other liqueur – between those who love it, and those who loathe it.

## Tricolor

- chilled green crème de menthe
- chilled Baileys Irish Cream
- chilled Grand Marnier

*Into a shot glass, pour the ingredients in sequence as gently as possible, so that each forms a distinct layer.*

## Tropical

- crème de cacao
- dry vermouth
- maraschino

dash Angostura bitters

dash orange bitters

*Stir over ice. Strain into a cocktail glass.*

## Union Jack 3

- maraschino
- blue curaçao
- grenadine

*For a patriotically striped cocktail, pour each ingredient in turn into a liqueur glass, being careful to avoid any mixing.*

## Unzip A Banana

- Baileys Irish Cream
- banana liqueur

*Stir over ice. Strain into a shot glass.*

## Upstairs

- Dubonnet
- lemon juice

soda water

*Pour Dubonnet and lemon juice into an ice-filled tumbler. Top with soda.*

---

Grand Marnier is named after Marnier Lapostolle, who created the liqueur in 1827. Lapostolle was a man of enormous wealth, but of diminutive stature. The story goes that he offered a sample of his new recipe to the hotelier César Ritz, asking him to suggest a suitable name for it. Ritz pronounced the drink delicious, and with the ingratiation instinctive in hotel managers, recommended *Grand* Marnier.

## Vie en Rose

- ⦂⦂ kirsch
- ⦂⦂ dry gin
- ⦂ grenadine
- ⦂ lemon juice

*Shake over ice. Strain into cocktail glasses.*

## Waldorf

- ⦂⦂ Swedish Punsch
- ⦂ dry gin
- ⦂ lemon juice

*Shake over ice. Strain into a cocktail glass.*

## Wedding Belle

- ⦂⦂ Dubonnet
- ⦂⦂ dry gin
- ⦂ cherry brandy
- ⦂ orange juice

*Shake over ice. Strain into cocktail glasses.*

## White Cloud

- ⦂⦂ Sambuca
- teaspoon lemon juice
- chilled sparkling water

*Pour Sambuca and lemon juice over ice in a tall glass. Top with sparkling water.*

## White Spider

- ⦂ crème de menthe
- ⦂ vodka

*Stir over ice. Strain into a cocktail glass.*

## Widow's Wish

- ⦂⦂ Bénédictine
- 1 egg
- fresh cream

*Shake Bénédictine and egg over ice. Strain into tumbler and top with cream.*

---

Bénédictine was first made by monks of the monastery at Fécamp in Normandy in 1510, but the original formula was lost when the monastery was destroyed during the French Revolution. Today's liqueur is from a recipe of 1863, but every bottle still carries the original Bénédictine dedication DOM: *Deo Optimo Maximo* – To God, Most Good, Most Great.

## Woo Woo

- ⚡ peach schnapps
- ⚡ vodka
- ⚡⚡ cranberry juice

*Shake over ice. Strain into a cocktail glass.*

## Xanthia

- ⚡ yellow Chartreuse
- ⚡ cherry brandy
- ⚡ dry gin

*Stir over ice. Strain into a cocktail glass.*

## Yellow Parrot

- ⚡ yellow Chartreuse
- ⚡ apricot brandy
- ⚡ pastis

*Stir over ice. Strain into a cocktail glass.*

## Yikes

- ⚡ amaretto
- ⚡ peach schnapps

*Shake over ice. Strain into a shot glass.*

## Yodel

- ⚡ Fernet Branca
- ⚡ orange juice
- soda water

*Stir Fernet and orange in a tumbler with ice. Top with soda.*

## Zaza

- ⚡⚡ Dubonnet
- ⚡ dry gin
- dash orange bitters

*Stir over ice. Strain into a cocktail glass.*

---

The ⚡ symbol in the recipes is a 'unit' to indicate proportions. A reasonable single measure to use in mixing is about an ounce – equivalent to 30 millilitres (ml). Quantities in the recipes given as dashes, spoonfuls etc., are based on one-ounce unit measures of the accompanying principal ingredients. A cocktail incorporating 2 to 3 measures of alcoholic ingredients makes a reasonably strong drink for one person. Cocktails with 4 or more measures are best made for two or more people.

# PORT & MADEIRA

Portugal's two fortified wines provide the essential ingredients for some delicious cocktails. Use inexpensive 'ruby' or 'tawny' ports for those recipes which specify nothing more particular. 'Late Bottled Vintage' and 'Vintage Character' ports are of better quality and could reasonably be expected to make a better cocktail, if expense is no object. Aged tawny (10 or 20 year old) port and vintage ports are made to be enjoyed as they are, and are far too subtle and expensive for mixing purposes. Madeira wines – from the Portuguese island of that name off the northwest African coast – have differing degrees of sweetness, according to the grape variety from which they are made. Driest is Sercial, followed by Verdelho, Bual and Malmsey in ascending order of sweetness. Sercial madeira is the customary wine for mixing.

## Atlantic

- ▮ Sandeman Ruby Port
- ▮ brandy
- 2 teaspoons crème du mure

*Shake over ice and pour over crushed ice in a stemmed glass. Add black cherry.*

*Creation of Dick Bradsall when barman at Atlantic Bar and Grill, London.*

## Baltimore Egg Nog

- ▮ madeira
- 4 dashes brandy
- 4 dashes rum
- ▮▮▮▮▮ milk
- 1 egg
- teaspoon sugar

*Shake over ice. Strain into stemmed glasses. Grate nutmeg over.*

## Brandy Madeira

▮▮ madeira

▮▮ brandy

▮ dry vermouth

*Stir over ice. Strain into cocktail glasses.*

## Broken Spur

▮▮▮▮ white port

▮ dry gin

▮ sweet vermouth

teaspoon Anisette

1 egg yolk

*Shake over ice. Strain into small wine glasses.*

## Choc Shock

▮▮▮ port

▮ yellow Chartreuse

teaspoon powdered chocolate

1 egg

*Shake over ice. Strain into a small wine glass.*

## Coffee

▮▮ port

▮ brandy

dash curaçao

teaspoon sugar

1 egg yolk

*Shake over ice. Strain into a cocktail glass and grate nutmeg over.*

*So named because of its appearance, not its taste.*

---

Mad Jack Mytton was a Shrewsbury squire who inherited a huge fortune of half a million pounds shortly before his 21st birthday in 1798. Like all the best Englishmen of his time, he hunted and feasted with equal appetite. A port enthusiast, he drank six bottles every day, turning to eau-de-Cologne when supplies ran dry. This made him prone to hiccoughs, which he attempted on one occasion to cure by setting himself on fire. He was mortally injured, but survived long enough to say, 'Well, by God, the hiccough is gone.'

## Devil's

- ▮ port
- ▮ dry vermouth
- 2 dashes lemon juice

*Shake over ice. Strain into a cocktail glass.*

## Diablo

- ▮▮▮ white port
- ▮▮ dry vermouth
- 4 dashes lemon juice

*Shake over ice. Strain into cocktail glasses.*

## Fizz & Chip

- ▮ Taylor's Chip Dry white port
- chilled tonic water

*Pour port into a tall glass and top with tonic. Add ice and a slice of lemon.*

*Traditional apéritif of Quinta de Vargellas, Taylor's beautiful estate in the Douro Valley, Portugal.*

## Madeira Mint Flip

- ▮▮ madeira
- ▮ chocolate mint liqueur
- 1 egg
- teaspoon grated plain chocolate

*Shake madeira, liqueur and egg over ice. Strain into cocktail glasses and sprinkle chocolate over.*

## New Orleans Punch

- ▮ Sandeman LBV Port
- ▮ brandy
- ▮ orange juice
- ▮ lemon juice
- 2 teaspoons sugar syrup
- soda water

*Shake over ice and pour into ice-filled tall tumblers. Top up with soda (or iced tea) and add lemon or orange slice.*

*Adapted by Dick Bradsall of Detroit bar, London, from a traditional recipe.*

'I'm very fortunate because I was born in 1931, a lousy year for every other wine, but the greatest year ever for Port, and people quite often give me bottles of Vintage 1931 for birthday presents.'
Sir Terence Conran

## Philadelphia Scotchman

▮ port

▮ apple brandy

▮ orange juice

dry ginger ale

*Shake over ice. Strain into a wine glass and top with ginger ale.*

## Port in a Storm

▮▮▮ port

▮ brandy

▮ lemon juice

*Stir over ice. Strain into small wine glasses.*

## Port Wine (1)

▮ port

dash brandy

*Stir over ice. Strain into a port glass.*

## Port Wine (2)

▮ port

2 dashes curaçao

dash Angostura bitters

dash orange bitters

*Stir over ice. Strain into a port glass.*

## Port Wine Flip

▮▮▮ port

1 egg

teaspoon sugar

pinch of nutmeg

*Shake port, egg and sugar over ice. Strain into a small wine glass and sprinkle nutmeg over.*

## Rainbow Room Coffee

⚫ port

⚫ brandy

small egg yolk

teaspoon sugar

*Shake over ice and strain into a cocktail glass.*

*There is no coffee in this recipe. The mixture looks like coffee with cream.*

## Savoy Sangaree

⚫ port

teaspoon caster sugar

pinch of nutmeg

*Stir port and sugar over ice. Strain into a cocktail glass and add nutmeg.*

*There is another Savoy Sangaree in the Sherry section.*

## Sevilla

⚫ port

⚫ rum

pinch of caster sugar

1 egg

*Shake over ice. Strain into a cocktail glass.*

## Tempter

⚫ port

⚫ apricot brandy

*Stir over ice. Strain into a cocktail glass.*

## Xerxes

⚫ white port

⚫⚫ tomato juice

dash Worcestershire sauce

*Shake over ice. Strain into a cocktail glass.*

An old gourmet who'd grown somewhat stout,
Felt a twinge and much feared it was gout.
'If I drink now,' he thought,
'Three whole bottles of port,
It surely will settle the doubt.'

Laurence Sterne

# RUM

The spirit of the Caribbean is said to owe its origins to Christopher Columbus, who planted the first sugar cane in the islands four hundred years ago. Spanish settlers who followed brought with them the art of distilling (learned from the Moors) and the sugar-based alcohol soon became the staple liquor of the New World. For mixing purposes use popular brands of white (clear) rum or dark rum. Flavours and weights do vary markedly from one producer to another, but most are equally suitable for cocktails. Where light or dark rums are suggested in the recipes here, it is according to the colour desired for the finished mix.

## Adam

- ▮▮ Jamaica rum
- ▮ grenadine
- ▮ fresh lemon juice

*Shake over ice. Strain into a cocktail glass.*

## Adios Amigos

- ▮▮ white rum
- ▮ cognac
- ▮ dry gin
- ▮ dry vermouth
- ▮ fresh lime juice

*Shake over ice. Strain into cocktail glasses.*

## Apple Pie

- ⚬ rum
- ⚬ sweet vermouth
- 2 dashes apple brandy
- 2 dashes lemon juice
- dash grenadine

*Shake over ice. Strain into a cocktail glass.*

## Bacardi Cocktail

- ⚬⚬ Bacardi rum
- ⚬ grenadine
- ⚬ fresh lime (or lemon) juice

*Shake over ice. Strain into a cocktail glass.*

## Back Bay

- ⚬⚬ rum
- ⚬ brandy
- 4 dashes peach brandy
- 2 dashes fresh lime juice

*Shake over ice. Strain into a cocktail glass.*

## Banana Cocktail

- ⚬ rum
- ⚬ banana liqueur
- ⚬ fresh cream
- 4 dashes orange juice
- dash Angostura bitters
- dash grenadine

*Shake all ingredients except grenadine over ice. Strain into an ice-filled tumbler and add grenadine.*

## Banana Colada

- ⚬⚬ rum
- ⚬⚬⚬⚬ pineapple juice
- ⚬ coconut liqueur
- 1 medium-sized banana, sliced

*Whizz in a blender with a handful of crushed ice. Serve in tall glasses with a straw.*

---

Men do not drink for the effect alcohol produces on the body. What they drink for is the brain-effect; and if it must come through the body, so much the worse for the body.

Jack London, *John Barleycorn*

## Banana Daiquiri

- ▮▮ rum
- ▮ Cointreau
- ▮ fresh lime juice
- 1 medium-sized banana, sliced

*Whizz in a blender with a handful of crushed ice. Serve in stemmed glasses with a straw.*

## Banana Rum

- ▮▮ rum
- ▮ banana liqueur
- ▮ orange juice

*Shake over ice. Strain into a cocktail glass.*

## Beachcomber

- ▮▮▮ rum
- ▮ Cointreau
- ▮ fresh lime juice
- 2 dashes grenadine
- sugar

*Encrust rims of cocktail glasses by dipping them in lime juice then in sugar. Shake liquid ingredients over ice and strain.*

## Bee's Knees

- ▮▮ rum
- 4 dashes Cointreau
- 2 dashes lemon juice
- teaspoon sugar

*Shake over ice. Strain into a cocktail glass.*

## Between-the-Sheets

- ▮ white rum
- ▮ brandy
- ▮ Cointreau
- ▮ lemon juice

*Shake over ice. Strain into shot glasses.*

## B52

- ▮▮ rum
- ▮ peach brandy
- ▮ dry vermouth

*Stir over ice. Strain into cocktail glasses.*

## Bishop

- ⚫ white rum
- teaspoon red wine
- dash lemon juice
- pinch sugar

*Stir over ice. Strain into a cocktail glass.*

## Black Devil

- ⚫ rum
- 4 dashes dry vermouth

*Stir over ice. Strain into a cocktail glass and add a black olive.*

## Blackout

- ⚫⚫ dark rum
- ⚫ Kahlúa
- 2 dashes lemon juice

*Shake over ice. Strain into an ice-filled tumbler.*

## Black Rose

- ⚫ rum
- teaspoon sugar
- chilled black coffee

*Dissolve sugar with rum in a tumbler. Add ice and top with coffee. Stir.*

## Blood Transfusion

- ⚫⚫ white rum
- ⚫ fresh lime juice
- dash grenadine

*Shake over ice. Strain into a cocktail glass.*

## Blue Hawaii

- ⚫ white rum
- ⚫ blue curaçao
- ⚫ coconut liqueur
- ⚫⚫ pineapple juice

*Shake over ice. Strain into ice-filled tumblers.*

## Blue Marlin

- ⚫⚫ white rum
- ⚫ blue curaçao
- ⚫⚫ fresh lime juice

*Shake over ice. Strain into shot glasses.*

## Bolero

- ⚫⚫ rum
- ⚫ apple brandy
- 2 dashes sweet vermouth

*Stir over ice. Strain into a cocktail glass.*

## Bolo

- ❚❚❚ rum
- ❚❚ orange juice
- ❚ lemon juice
- teaspoon sugar

*Shake over ice. Strain into cocktail glasses.*

## Bossanova

- ❚ rum
- ❚ Galliano
- teaspoon apricot brandy
- ❚❚❚ pineapple juice

*Shake over ice. Strain into tall glasses.*

## Boston Cooler

- ❚❚ rum
- ❚ lemon juice
- teaspoon sugar
- chilled ginger ale

*Shake rum, lemon and sugar over ice. Strain into an ice-filled tall glass. Top with soda and add a lemon slice.*

## Buck Jones

- ❚❚ white rum
- ❚ sweet sherry
- ❚ fresh lime juice
- chilled dry ginger ale

*Shake rum, sherry and lime over ice. Strain into ice-filled tumblers and top with ginger ale.*

---

The ❚ symbol in the recipes is a 'unit' to indicate proportions. A reasonable single measure to use in mixing is about an ounce – equivalent to 30 millilitres (ml). Quantities in the recipes given as dashes, spoonfuls etc., are based on one-ounce unit measures of the accompanying principal ingredients. A cocktail incorporating 2 to 3 measures of alcoholic ingredients makes a reasonably strong drink for one person. Cocktails with 4 or more measures are best made for two or more people.

## Bush Baby

- white rum
- Capéritif
- 2 dashes Angostura bitters

*Stir over ice. Strain into a cocktail glass.*

## Bush Ranger

- rum
- Dubonnet
- dash Angostura bitters

*Stir over ice. Strain into a cocktail glass.*

## BVD

- Bacardi white rum
- dry gin
- dry vermouth

*Stir over ice. Strain into a cocktail glass.*

*The initials originally signified brandy, vermouth and Dubonnet, but this recipe is the current version.*

## Caparina

- cachaca (Brazilian cane spirit)
- half a lime
- 2 teaspoons sugar

*Chop lime into four pieces and place in a tumbler. Add sugar, and crush fruit with a pestle or spoon. Add spirit and crushed ice. Stir.*

## Caribe

- rum
- orange juice
- lemon juice
- 2 teaspoons sugar

*Shake over ice. Strain into cocktail glasses.*

## Casa Blanca

- rum
- 2 dashes Cointreau
- 2 dashes maraschino
- 2 dashes fresh lime juice

*Shake over ice. Strain into a cocktail glass.*

## Cherie

- ❚❚ white rum
- ❚ cherry brandy
- ❚ triple sec
- ❚ fresh lime juice

*Shake over ice. Strain into cocktail glasses and add a maraschino cherry.*

## Cherry Rum

- ❚❚ rum
- ❚ cherry brandy
- ❚ fresh cream

*Shake over ice. Strain into cocktail glasses.*

## Chinese

- ❚❚ rum
- ❚ grenadine
- 3 dashes curaçao
- 3 dashes maraschino
- dash Angostura bitters

*Shake over ice. Strain into a cocktail glass.*

## Chiquita

- ❚❚❚ rum
- ❚ banana liqueur
- ❚❚ fresh cream
- 2 dashes grenadine

*Shake over ice. Strain into cocktail glasses.*

## Chocolate Rum

- ❚❚ white rum
- ❚ crème de cacao
- ❚ crème de menthe
- 2 teaspoons fresh cream

*Shake over ice. Strain into cocktail glasses.*

## Cinderella

- ❚❚❚ rum
- ❚ port
- ❚ lemon juice
- 1 egg white
- teaspoon sugar syrup

*Shake over ice. Strain into cocktail glasses.*

I have made an important discovery – that alcohol taken in sufficient quantities produces all the effects of intoxication.

Oscar Wilde

## Cocomacoque

- ⵣ white rum
- ⵣ orange juice
- ⵣ pineapple juice
- ⵣⵣ red wine

*Shake rum and juices over ice. Strain into an ice-filled wine glass and add wine. Stir to mix.*

## Columbia

- ⵣⵣ rum
- ⵣ raspberry syrup
- ⵣ lemon juice

*Shake over ice. Strain into cocktail glasses.*

## Continental

- ⵣⵣⵣ white rum
- ⵣ crème de menthe
- ⵣ fresh lime juice
- teaspoon caster sugar

*Shake over ice. Strain into cocktail glasses.*

## Corkscrew

- ⵣⵣⵣ rum
- ⵣ peach brandy
- ⵣ dry vermouth

*Stir over ice. Strain into cocktail glasses.*

## Cream Puff

- ⵣⵣ white rum
- ⵣ fresh cream
- teaspoon caster sugar
- chilled soda water

*Shake rum, cream and sugar. Strain into a wine glass. Top with soda and stir.*

## Creole

- ⵣ rum
- 4 dashes lemon juice
- dash Tabasco
- chilled beef consommé

*Shake rum, lemon and Tabasco over ice. Strain into an ice-filled tumbler and top with consommé. Season with salt and pepper to taste.*

## Cuba

- ⚫⚫ white rum
- ⚫ fresh lime juice
- half teaspoon sugar

*Shake over ice. Strain into a cocktail glass.*

## Cuba Libre

- ⚫⚫ Bacardi rum
- ⚫ fresh lime juice
- Coca-Cola

*Shake rum and lime juice over ice. Strain into an ice-filled glass and top up with Cola.*

## Cuban Special

- ⚫⚫ rum
- ⚫ fresh lime juice
- ⚫ pineapple juice
- teaspoon triple sec

*Shake over ice. Strain into cocktail glasses.*

## Culross

- ⚫ rum
- ⚫ apricot brandy
- ⚫ Lillet
- ⚫ lemon juice

*Shake over ice. Strain into a cocktail glass.*

*Aficionados of this drink pronounce it 'Koorrus'.*

## Daiquiri

- ⚫⚫⚫ rum
- ⚫ fresh lime juice
- teaspoon sugar

*Shake over ice. Strain into cocktail glasses.*

*There are limitless variations on the Daiquiri theme involving flavourings and the addition of egg white. Daiquiri is a town in Cuba, where the drink is said to have been first devised around 1900.*

---

A fastidious Canadian doctor was in the habit of enjoying a daiquiri in the same bar on the stroke of one o'clock every weekday lunchtime. He liked the drink flavoured with a little nutmeg. On one occasion, he noticed it tasted quite different from usual.

'What the hell have you done to my daiquiri?' he demanded.

The barman replied that he'd run out of nutmeg and had substituted another flavouring: 'It's a hickory daiquiri, doc.'

## Dark & Stormy

- ∎ rum
- ∎∎ ginger beer

*Combine in an ice-filled tumbler.*

## Derby 2

- ∎∎ rum
- ∎ orange juice
- 4 dashes Cointreau
- 2 dashes fresh lime juice

*Shake over ice. Strain into a cocktail glass.*

## Devil's Tail

- ∎∎∎ rum
- ∎∎ vodka
- ∎ fresh lime juice
- 4 dashes apricot brandy
- 2 dashes grenadine

*Shake over ice. Strain into cocktail glasses.*

## Dunlop

- ∎∎ rum
- ∎ dry sherry
- dash Angostura bitters

*Stir over ice. Strain into a cocktail glass.*

## El Presidente

- ∎∎ rum
- ∎ fresh lime juice
- ∎ curaçao
- dash Angostura bitters

*Shake over ice. Strain into a cocktail glass.*

---

It was a capital thing for preserving the dead admiral when they put him into a rum puncheon; but it was a bad thing for the sailors when they tapped the cask and drank the liquor, till they had left the admiral, as he had never left his ship, high and dry.

Dr Guthrie, *The Temperance Handbook*

## Eye Opener

▮ rum

2 dashes crème de noyaux

2 dashes curaçao

2 dashes pastis

teaspoon sugar

1 egg yolk

*Shake over ice. Strain into a cocktail glass.*

## Fair and Warmer

▮▮ rum

▮ sweet vermouth

2 dashes curaçao

*Stir over ice. Strain into a cocktail glass.*

## Fireman's Lift

▮▮ rum

▮ fresh lime juice

4 dashes grenadine

sprinkling of sugar

*Shake over ice. Strain into a cocktail glass and add a maraschino cherry.*

## Florida Rum

▮▮ rum

▮ grapefruit juice

3 dashes dry vermouth

3 dashes sweet vermouth

*Shake over ice. Strain into a cocktail glass.*

## Fog Lifter

▮▮▮ rum

▮ brandy

▮ dry gin

▮ orange juice

▮ madeira

*Shake all but the madeira over ice. Strain into ice-filled tumblers and add madeira.*

## Four Flush

▮▮ Bacardi rum

▮ dry vermouth

▮ Swedish Punsch

dash grenadine

*Stir over ice. Strain into cocktail glasses.*

## Fox Trot

> ▌ Bacardi rum

teaspoon fresh lime juice

dash orange curaçao

*Shake over ice. Strain into a cocktail glass.*

## Framboise

> ▌▌ rum
>
> ▌ crème de framboise
>
> ▌ fresh cream

*Shake over ice. Strain into cocktail glasses.*

*Raspberries and cream in a glass.*

## Full House

> ▌▌ Bacardi rum
>
> ▌ dry vermouth
>
> ▌ Swedish Punsch

*Shake over ice. Strain into cocktail glasses.*

## Gauguin

> ▌▌ rum
>
> ▌ mixed fresh lime and lemon juice

teaspoon passionfruit syrup

*Shake over ice. Strain into a small wine glass and add a maraschino cherry.*

## Golden Gate 2

> ▌▌ rum
>
> ▌ dry gin
>
> ▌ crème de cacao
>
> ▌ lemon juice

pinch of dried ginger

*Shake over ice. Strain into cocktail glasses and add orange slices.*

## Gradeal Special

> ▌▌ rum
>
> ▌ apricot brandy
>
> ▌ dry gin

*Stir over ice. Strain into cocktail glasses.*

## Grand Bahama

- ▮▮ rum
- ▮ brandy
- ▮ Cointreau
- ▮▮ fresh lime juice

*Shake over ice. Strain into cocktail glasses.*

## Grog

- ▮▮ rum
- ▮▮ boiling water
- lemon slice
- pinch of cinnamon
- teaspoon sugar
- 4 cloves

*Shake all but water and strain into a sturdy stemmed glass. Add boiling water.*

*Commemorates the order made by British Admiral Edward 'Old Grog' Vernon in 1740 that the rum rations given daily to sailors should thenceforth be watered in the interests of economy and sobriety.*

## Havana Ron

- ▮ rum
- ▮ pineapple juice
- dash lemon juice

*Shake over ice. Strain into a cocktail glass.*

## Hibiscus

- ▮ rum
- 4 dashes fresh lime juice
- dash grenadine

*Shake over ice. Strain into a cocktail glass.*

## Hop Cane Toad

- ▮ rum
- ▮ apricot brandy
- 2 dashes fresh lime juice

*Shake over ice. Strain into a cocktail glass.*

## Hot Rum with Butter

- ✶ rum
- ✶✶✶ boiling water
- dessertspoon butter
- quarter cinnamon stick
- a clove
- lemon slice
- half teaspoon sugar
- pinch nutmeg

*Warm a coffee mug and add the sugar, cinnamon and cloves. Add boiling water then the butter and rum. Stir and add lemon slice and nutmeg.*

## Hotcha

- ✶✶ rum
- ✶ dry sherry

*Stir over ice. Strain into a cocktail glass.*

## Hurricane

- ✶✶ rum
- ✶✶ fresh lime juice
- ✶ passionfruit syrup

*Shake over ice. Strain into cocktail glasses.*

## Jacqueline

- ✶✶ dark rum
- ✶ triple sec
- ✶ fresh lime juice
- pinch caster sugar

*Shake over ice. Strain into a cocktail glass.*

## Jade

- ✶✶✶ rum
- ✶ Cointreau
- ✶ crème de menthe
- ✶ fresh lime juice
- teaspoon sugar

*Shake over ice. Strain into cocktail glasses.*

## Jamaica

- ✶ Jamaican rum
- ✶ Tia Maria
- ✶ fresh lime juice
- dash Angostura bitters

*Shake over ice. Strain into a cocktail glass.*

## Jo'burg

- ⧗ rum
- ⧗ Capéritif
- 4 dashes orange bitters

*Stir over ice. Strain into a cocktail glass and squeeze lemon peel over.*

## Junkanoo

- ⧗⧗ rum
- 4 dashes peach brandy
- 4 dashes curaçao
- 2 dashes fresh lime juice
- dash orange bitters

*Shake over ice. Strain into a cocktail glass.*

## Kempinski

- ⧗ rum
- ⧗ Cointreau
- ⧗⧗ grapefruit juice

*Shake over ice. Strain into a cocktail glass and add a maraschino cherry.*

*From the Bristol Kempinski hotel, Berlin.*

## Kicker

- ⧗⧗ rum
- ⧗ apple brandy
- 2 dashes sweet vermouth

*Stir over ice. Strain into a cocktail glass.*

---

From the earliest days of Britain's Royal Navy, founded by Henry VIII in the 1530s, a daily ration of half a pint of rum was issued to all sailors. The practice continued for two hundred years until Admiral Edward Vernon ordered that the spirit be diluted with water before issue. The diminished ration became known as 'grog' after the admiral's nickname of Old Grog, deriving from the distinctive, non-regulation cloak Vernon wore at all times. The garment was made from grogram, a coarse fabric woven from mohair, silk and wool. The official naval rum ration was finally discontinued in 1969.

## Kingston

**▪▪** rum

**▪** kümmel

**▪** orange juice

dash Pimento Dram

*Shake over ice. Strain into a cocktail glass.*

## Knickerbocker Special

**▪** rum

teaspoon lemon juice

teaspoon orange juice

teaspoon raspberry syrup

2 dashes curaçao

*Shake over ice. Strain into a cocktail glass.*

## Leeward

**▪▪▪** rum

**▪** apple brandy

**▪** sweet vermouth

dash grenadine

*Stir over ice. Strain into cocktail glasses.*

## Limey

**▪▪** rum

**▪▪** Rose's lime juice cordial

**▪** Cointreau

**▪** fresh lime juice

*Shake over ice. Strain into small wine glasses part-filled with crushed ice. Add lime slices.*

## Little Princess

**▪** rum

**▪** sweet vermouth

*Stir over ice. Strain into a cocktail glass and squeeze lemon peel over.*

## Lounge Lizard

**▪▪** dark rum

**▪** amaretto

chilled cola

*Pour spirits into an ice-filled tall glass. Top with cola and stir.*

## Mai Tai

∎∎∎ rum

∎ apricot brandy

∎ curaçao

∎ fresh lime juice

4 dashes grenadine

*Shake over ice. Strain into cocktail glasses and add maraschino cherries.*

*Attributed to Trader Vic of the eponymous bar-restaurant in Oakland, California, USA.*

## Mallorca

∎∎ rum

∎ banana liqueur

∎ Drambuie

∎ dry vermouth

*Stir over ice. Strain into cocktail glasses.*

## Malmaison

∎∎ rum

∎ sweet sherry

∎ lemon juice

dash Anisette

*Shake over ice. Strain into a cocktail glass.*

## Mañana

∎∎∎ rum

∎ apricot brandy

4 dashes lemon juice

*Shake over ice. Strain into cocktail glasses.*

## Mary Pickford

∎ rum

∎ pineapple juice

2 dashes grenadine

*Shake over ice. Strain into a cocktail glass.*

*Named after the American actress and film producer, née Gladys Mary Smith, (1893-1979).*

## Melba

∎∎ rum

∎∎ Swedish Punsch

4 dashes lemon juice

dash grenadine

dash pastis

*Shake over ice. Strain into cocktail glasses.*

## Miami

- ❚❚ rum
- ❚ crème de menthe
- dash lemon juice

*Shake over ice. Strain into a cocktail glass.*

## Midnight Express

- ❚❚ dark rum
- ❚ Cointreau
- ❚❚ fresh lime juice

*Shake over ice. Strain into cocktail glasses.*

## Millionaire

- ❚ rum
- ❚ apricot brandy
- ❚ sloe gin
- ❚ fresh lime juice
- dash grenadine

*Shake over ice. Strain into a cocktail glass.*

## Monkey Wrench

- ❚❚ white rum
- grapefruit juice

*Pour rum over ice in a tall glass. Top with grapefruit juice and stir.*

## Montego Bay

- ❚ Jamaican rum
- ❚ mixed fresh lime and pineapple juice
- dash grenadine

*Shake over ice. Strain into a cocktail glass.*

## Mojito

- ❚❚ rum
- ❚ fresh lime juice
- dash Angostura bitters
- teaspoon sugar
- mint sprig

*Shake over ice. Strain into a cocktail glass.*

# Navy

- ▮▮▮ dark rum
- ▮ sweet vermouth
- ▮ orange juice

*Shake over ice. Strain into cocktail glasses.*

# Nawlins

- ▮▮ rum
- ▮ mixed fresh lime and orange juice

chilled dry ginger ale

*Shake rum and fruit juice over ice. Strain into ice-filled tumblers and top with ginger ale.*

*Name marks New Orleans origin of this recipe.*

# Nevada

- ▮▮▮ Bacardi rum
- ▮▮ grapefruit juice
- ▮ fresh lime juice

dash Angostura bitters

*Shake over ice. Strain into cocktail glasses.*

# Palm Beach

- ▮ Bacardi rum
- ▮ dry gin
- ▮ pineapple juice

*Shake over ice. Strain into a cocktail glass.*

# Palmetto

- ▮ rum
- ▮ sweet vermouth

2 dashes orange bitters

*Stir over ice. Strain into a cocktail glass.*

# Panama

- ▮ rum
- ▮ crème de cacao
- ▮ fresh cream

*Shake over ice. Strain into a cocktail glass.*

# Panama Hat

- ▮▮▮ rum
- ▮▮ banana liqueur
- ▮ curaçao

teaspoon lemon juice

*Shake over ice. Strain into cocktail glasses.*

## Parisian Blonde

- rum
- curaçao
- sweetened fresh cream

*Shake over ice. Strain into a cocktail glass.*

## Pauline

- rum
- lemon juice

2 dashes pastis

pinch of sugar

pinch of nutmeg

*Shake over ice. Strain into a cocktail glass.*

## Peaches and Cream

- rum
- peach brandy

tablespoon fresh cream

*Shake over ice. Strain into a cocktail glass.*

## Petite Fleur

- rum
- Cointreau
- grapefruit juice

dash grenadine

*Shake over ice. Strain into a cocktail glass.*

## Piña Colada

- rum
- coconut liqueur
- pineapple juice

*Shake over ice. Strain into ice-filled tumblers and add fresh (not canned) pineapple slices if available.*

*A variation is to substitute coconut milk for the coconut liqueur.*

## Pink Planter

- white rum
- coconut liqueur
- amaretto
- cranberry juice
- pineapple juice

*Shake over ice. Strain into tall, ice-filled glasses.*

## Planter's Cocktail

- ▮ rum
- ▮ orange juice
- dash lemon juice

*Shake over ice. Strain into a cocktail glass.*

## Planter's Punch 1

- ▮▮ Jamaica rum
- ▮ fresh lime juice
- teaspoon sugar
- dash Angostura bitters

*Shake over ice. Strain into a tall ice-filled glass and add fruit slices.*

## Planter's Punch 2

- ▮▮ Jamaica rum
- ▮ fresh lime juice
- ▮ lemon juice
- ▮ orange juice
- teaspoon pineapple juice
- teaspoon triple sec
- 2 dashes grenadine

*Stir rum and fruit juices in a tall glass filled with ice cubes. Add triple sec and grenadine and stir gently. Add a slice each of lemon, orange and pineapple.*

Rum distilling was a major industry in the New England of the early eighteenth century, until Parliament in London passed a Molasses Act in 1733, imposing high taxes on sugar imports from outside the British empire. The first rebellions by American colonists protesting 'No taxation without representation' were in response to the act and, in effect, the beginnings of the struggle for independence.

## Platinum Blonde

- ▮▮ rum
- ▮▮ Cointreau
- ▮ fresh cream

*Shake over ice. Strain into cocktail glasses.*

## Poker

- ▮ Bacardi rum
- ▮ sweet vermouth

*Stir over ice. Strain into a cocktail glass.*

## Polynesia

- ▮▮ rum
- ▮▮ passionfruit juice
- ▮ fresh lime juice
- dash Angostura bitters
- 1 egg white

*Shake over ice. Strain into small wine glasses.*

## President

- ▮▮ rum
- ▮ orange juice
- 2 dashes grenadine

*Shake over ice. Strain into a cocktail glass.*

## Professor Saintsbury's Punch

- ▮▮▮ rum
- ▮▮ brandy
- ▮ lemon juice
- ▮▮▮▮▮ hot water
- sugar to taste

*Combine in a punch bowl and serve warm in small wine glasses.*

*'I never knew this mixture find fault with respectable persons of any age, sex, or condition, from undergraduates to old ladies, at any hour between sunset and sunrise,' claimed Prof George Saintsbury in Notes on a Cellar-Book in 1920.*

## Quaker's

- ▮▮ rum
- ▮▮ brandy
- ▮ lemon juice
- ▮ raspberry syrup

*Stir over ice. Strain into a cocktail glass.*

## Quarter Deck

▮▮ rum

▮ dry sherry

4 dashes fresh lime juice

*Shake over ice. Strain into a cocktail glass.*

## Queen of Spades

▮▮ rum

▮ Tia Maria

▮ fresh cream

*Shake over ice. Strain into cocktail glasses.*

## Red Flag

▮ rum

▮ dry gin

▮ pineapple juice

dash grenadine

*Shake over ice. Strain into a cocktail glass.*

## Robson

▮▮ rum

▮ grenadine

▮ lemon and orange juice

*Shake over ice. Strain into cocktail glasses.*

## Roman Road

▮ rum

▮ brandy

▮ lemon juice

teaspoon raspberry syrup

*Shake over ice. Strain into a cocktail glass.*

## Rumartini

▮ chilled rum

dash chilled dry vermouth

*Combine in a cocktail glass with an ice cube. Squeeze lemon peel over.*

## Rum Cocktail

▮▮ rum

▮ sweet vermouth

*Stir over ice. Strain into a cocktail glass.*

## Rum Collins

▮▮ white rum

▮ fresh lime juice

teaspoon caster sugar

soda water

*Shake rum, lime and sugar over ice. Strain into a tall, ice-filled glass and top with soda.*

## Rum Daisy

- ✶✶ rum
- ✶✶ lemon juice
- ✶ raspberry syrup

*Shake over ice. Strain into ice-filled tumblers and add lemon slices.*

## Rum Fix

- ✶✶ rum
- ✶ lemon juice
- teaspoon sugar
- dash grenadine

*Shake over ice. Strain into a tall, ice-filled glass and add a lemon slice.*

## Rum Punch

- 1 bottle rum
- 1 bottle brandy
- juice of 10 lemons
- 3 tablespoons sugar

*Combine in a punch bowl.*

*If serving cold, chill all ingredients beforehand and add 1 litre chilled sparkling water and ice. For hot punch add 2 pints (1 litre) boiling water. Add fruit slices.*

## Rum Tee Tum

- ✶✶ rum
- ✶ Cointreau
- 2 dashes Angostura bitters

*Stir over ice. Strain into a cocktail glass.*

---

The ✶ symbol in the recipes is a 'unit' to indicate proportions. A reasonable single measure to use in mixing is about an ounce – equivalent to 30 millilitres (ml). Quantities in the recipes given as dashes, spoonfuls etc., are based on one-ounce unit measures of the accompanying principal ingredients. A cocktail incorporating 2 to 3 measures of alcoholic ingredients makes a reasonably strong drink for one person. Cocktails with 4 or more measures are best made for two or more people.

## Rum Yellowbird

▮ ▮ rum

4 dashes Cointreau

4 dashes Galliano

2 dashes lime juice

*Shake over ice. Strain into a tall tumbler filled with crushed ice and serve with a straw.*

## Santiago

▮ Bacardi rum

2 dashes grenadine

2 dashes lemon juice

*Shake over ice. Strain into a cocktail glass.*

## Saxon

▮ ▮ rum

▮ fresh lime juice

dash grenadine

*Shake over ice. Strain into a cocktail glass.*

## Scorpion

▮ ▮ rum

▮ brandy

▮ ▮ mixed lemon and orange juice

2 dashes curaçao

*Shake over ice. Strain into ice-filled tumblers and add orange slices.*

## September Morn

▮ ▮ rum

▮ sweet vermouth

strip orange peel

*Shake over ice. Strain into a cocktail glass.*

## Sevilla

▮ rum

▮ dry gin

▮ pineapple juice

dash grenadine

*Shake over ice. Strain into a cocktail glass.*

## Shanghai

▮▮ rum

▮ lemon juice

4 dashes Anisette

dash grenadine

*Shake over ice. Strain into a cocktail glass.*

## Silver Bells

▮ rum

▮ dry gin

▮ lemon juice

2 dashes crème de noyaux

*Shake over ice. Strain into a cocktail glass.*

## Sir Walter

▮ rum

▮ brandy

4 dashes curaçao

4 dashes grenadine

4 dashes lemon juice

*Shake over ice. Strain into a cocktail glass.*

## Sonora

▮ rum

▮ apple brandy

2 dashes apricot brandy

dash lemon juice

*Shake over ice. Strain into a cocktail glass.*

## Spanish Main

▮▮▮ rum

▮ curaçao

3 dashes fresh lime juice

*Shake over ice. Strain into a cocktail glass.*

## Spanish Town

▮ rum

2 dashes triple sec

*Stir over ice. Strain into a cocktail glass.*

## Stanley

- ▮▮ rum
- ▮▮ dry gin
- ▮ lemon juice
- ▮ grenadine

*Shake over ice. Strain into cocktail glasses.*

## Sunflower

- ▮▮▮ rum
- ▮ Cointreau
- ▮ mixed lemon and orange juice

dash orange bitters

*Shake over ice. Strain into cocktail glasses.*

## Sunshine Special

- ▮▮ rum
- ▮▮ dry vermouth
- ▮ lemon juice

2 dashes crème de cassis

*Shake over ice. Strain into cocktail glasses.*

## Sylvie

- ▮▮ rum
- ▮ dry vermouth
- ▮▮ orange juice

dash amaretto

*Shake over ice. Strain into cocktail glasses.*

## Tanglefoot

- ▮▮ rum
- ▮▮ Swedish Punsch
- ▮ lemon juice
- ▮ orange juice

*Shake over ice. Strain into cocktail glasses.*

## Tarantella

- ▮ rum
- ▮ Strega

*Stir over ice. Strain into a cocktail glass and squeeze lemon peel over.*

## Third Rail

- rum
- apple brandy
- brandy
  dash pastis

*Shake over ice. Strain into a cocktail glass.*

## Tobago

- rum
- dry gin
- fresh lime juice
  dash curaçao

*Shake over ice. Strain into a cocktail glass.*

## Toby Special

- Bacardi rum
- apricot brandy
- grenadine
- lemon juice

*Shake over ice. Strain into a cocktail glass.*

## Tom & Jerry

- rum
- brandy
  teaspoon sugar
  1 egg white, beaten
  1 egg yolk, beaten

*Mix in a large wine glass and top with boiling water. Sprinkle nutmeg over.*

---

Lady Cunard's butler was blatantly the worse for drink on duty at a particularly grand formal dinner. The hostess hurriedly wrote him a note: 'You are drunk. Go to bed at once.' With an imperious eye, she summoned him to her place at the head of the table and handed him the piece of paper. He read it with solemn attention, walked around the table, and handed the note to Austen Chamberlain, the Foreign Secretary. He in turn read the note, left the table and went home.

## Torridora

- ▌▌ rum
- ▌ Kahlúa
- ▌ chilled fresh cream

*Shake over ice. Strain into a cocktail glass.*

## Trade Winds

- ▌ rum
- teaspoon sloe gin
- teaspoon fresh lime juice
- sprinkle of sugar

*Shake over ice. Strain into a cocktail glass.*

## Tropica

- ▌ rum
- ▌▌▌ pineapple juice
- ▌ grapefruit juice
- dash grenadine

*Shake over ice. Strain into an ice-filled tumbler.*

## Twelve Miles Out

- ▌ rum
- ▌ apple brandy
- ▌ Swedish Punsch

*Shake over ice. Strain into a cocktail glass and squeeze orange peel over.*

## White Lily

- ▌ rum
- ▌ Cointreau
- ▌ dry gin
- dash pastis

*Stir over ice. Strain into a cocktail glass.*

## White Lion

- ▌▌ rum
- ▌ lemon juice
- dash Angostura bitters
- dash grenadine
- teaspoon sugar

*Shake over ice. Strain into a cocktail glass.*

## XYZ

- ▮▮ rum
- ▮ Cointreau
- ▮ lemon juice

*Shake over ice. Strain into a cocktail glass.*

## Yacht Club

- ▮▮ rum
- ▮ lemon juice
- 2 dashes pastis
- 2 dashes grenadine
- soda water

*Shake all but the soda over ice. Strain into an ice-filled tall glass and top with soda.*

## Zamba

- ▮▮▮ rum
- ▮ lemon juice
- 2 dashes sweet vermouth
- dash Angostura bitters

*Shake over ice. Strain into a cocktail glass.*

## Zee Rons

- ▮ white rum
- ▮ dark rum
- ▮ fresh lime juice
- dash Cointreau

*Shake over ice. Strain into a shot glass.*

## Zombie

- ▮▮▮ rum
- ▮ apricot brandy
- ▮ fresh lime juice
- ▮ pineapple juice
- teaspoon sugar

*Shake over ice. Strain into ice-filled tall glasses. Add an orange slice and maraschino cherry to each.*

# SHERRY

The great fortified wine of Spain's southernmost province, Andalusia, was the world's most widely exported alcoholic drink until the twentieth century. The first era of the cocktail, the early 1900s, coincides exactly with the fall in sherry's fortunes. But sherry – so-named after its principal town of origin, Jerez – continues to hold its own in Europe and the United States, where its infinite variety and consistent quality still earn it the justified affection of devoted aficionados. True sherries are all dry, but this century has seen the introduction of 'medium' wines made to appeal to an imagined market with a sweeter tooth. These wines have no appeal to true lovers of the wine of Jerez, but are fine for chilling and mixing as components of cocktails.

## Adonis

▮▮ fino or manzanilla sherry

▮ sweet vermouth

dash orange bitters

*Stir over ice. Strain into a cocktail glass and squeeze orange peel over.*

## Balm

▮ sherry

4 dashes Cointreau

4 dashes orange juice

dash orange bitters

dash Pimento Dram Liqueur

*Shake over ice. Strain into cocktail glasses.*

## Bamboo

- ▮▮ dry sherry
- ▮ dry vermouth
- ▮ sweet vermouth

*Stir over ice. Strain into a cocktail glass.*

## Brazil

- ▮ dry sherry
- ▮ dry vermouth
- dash pastis
- dash Angostura bitters

*Stir over ice. Strain into a cocktail glass.*

## Cadiz

- ▮ dry sherry
- ▮ blackberry liqueur
- ▮ equal mix of Cointreau and fresh cream

*Shake over ice. Strain into a cocktail glass.*

## Coronation Salute

- ▮ dry sherry
- ▮ dry vermouth
- 2 dashes orange bitters
- dash maraschino

*Shake over ice. Strain into a cocktail glass.*

## Creamy Orange

- ▮▮ 'cream' (sweet) sherry
- ▮▮ orange juice
- ▮ brandy
- ▮ fresh cream

*Shake over ice. Strain into cocktail glasses.*

## Cupid

- ▮▮ dry sherry
- teaspoon sugar
- 1 egg
- drop Tabasco

*Shake over ice. Strain into a cocktail glass.*

---

Sherry's great popularity in England dates from 1587, the year in which Sir Francis Drake made a daring raid on the Armada being prepared at Cadiz. Drake not only destroyed the Spanish fleet, but seized 2,900 barrels of sherry from the quayside, loaded them into captured galleons, and sailed home in triumph. The booty was sold for high prices in London, and the fashion for 'sack' was launched.

## Duke of Marlborough

- ▮ dry sherry
- ▮ sweet vermouth
- 2 dashes orange bitters

*Stir over ice. Strain into a cocktail glass and add an orange peel twist.*

## East Indian

- ▮ dry sherry
- ▮ dry vermouth
- dash orange bitters

*Shake over ice. Strain into a cocktail glass.*

## Fandango

- ▮▮ dry sherry
- ▮ rum
- dash orange bitters

*Stir over ice. Strain into a cocktail glass.*

## Greenbriar

- ▮▮ dry sherry
- ▮ dry vermouth
- dash peach bitters
- sprig fresh mint

*Stir over ice. Strain into a cocktail glass.*

## Harveys Wallhanger

- ▮ Harveys Bristol Cream
- ▮ rum
- ▮▮ tomato juice
- sprinkle of black pepper

*Shake over ice. Strain into a small wine glass.*

## Negus

- 1 bottle dark sherry
- 2 pints (1 litre) boiling water
- 1 lemon, sliced
- sherry glass of brandy
- 1 or 2 teaspoons sugar
- nutmeg

*Warm the sherry in a saucepan before adding the boiling water and lemon slices. Take the pan off the heat and add the brandy. Sweeten to taste with the sugar and grate nutmeg over. Serve in sturdy small wine glasses.*

*Port can be substituted for sherry.*

*The drink is named after Francis Negus, a keen aficionado who died in 1732.*

## Nice Pair

- ⚱ dry sherry
- ⚱ cream sherry
- ⚱ rum
- 2 dashes orange bitters

*Shake over ice. Strain into a small wine glass.*

*Purists make this cocktail with Harveys of Bristol sherries – namely Bristol Cream and Bristol Milk.*

## Philomel

- ⚱⚱⚱ dry sherry
- ⚱⚱ orange juice
- ⚱ quinquina
- ⚱ rum
- sprinkling of freshly ground pepper

*Shake over ice. Strain into small wine glasses.*

## Picador

- ⚱⚱ dry sherry
- 3 dashes Cointreau

*Stir over ice in a large sherry glass and squeeze lemon peel over.*

## Reform

- ⚱⚱ dry sherry
- ⚱ dry vermouth
- dash orange bitters

*Stir over ice. Strain into a cocktail glass.*

## Roc-a-Coe

- ⚱ dry sherry
- ⚱ dry gin

*Stir over ice. Strain into a cocktail glass and add a maraschino cherry.*

---

Captain Thomas Harvey, father of the founder of the famed Bristol sherry company (est. 1796), was a seafarer with a fearsome reputation for holding his drink. Ashore in Bristol he once drank a companion, literally, under the table. Harvey summoned his servant. 'Kindly remove Mr Prothero,' he commanded, 'and bring me another bottle of port.'

## Savoy Sangaree 2

▨ sherry

teaspoon caster sugar

pinch of nutmeg

*Stir sherry and sugar over ice. Strain into a cocktail glass and add nutmeg.*

## Sherry Cocktail

▨ dry sherry

2 dashes dry vermouth

2 dashes orange bitters

*Stir over ice. Strain into a cocktail glass.*

## Ship

▨▨ sherry

▨ rum

▨ whisky

▨ prune syrup

*Shake over ice. Strain into cocktail glasses.*

## Up-to-Date

▨ dry sherry

▨ rye whiskey

dash Angostura bitters

dash Grand Marnier

*Stir over ice. Strain into a cocktail glass.*

## Utility

▨▨ sherry

▨ dry vermouth

▨ sweet sherry

*Stir over ice. Strain into a sherry or cocktail glass.*

## Xeres

▨ dry sherry

dash orange bitters

dash peach bitters

*Stir over ice. Strain into a sherry or cocktail glass.*

Banking and wine-trading were two of the great moneyspinners of the nineteenth century. Members of the Sandeman family, of port and sherry fame, include the founder of the Bank of Scotland, and a Governor of the Bank of England. The present head of Sandeman in Oporto, George Sandeman, is from the seventh successive generation of his family to work in the business since it was founded by George Sandeman in 1790.

# TEQUILA

Mexico's national spirit has enjoyed burgeoning popularity on both sides of the Atlantic as the central ingredient in cocktails such as the classic Margarita and the sticky Tequila Sunrise. Distilled from a sort of beer called *pulque* – brewed from the succulent agave plant, a relation of the cactus – tequila enjoys a mythical reputation for potency. Commercial brands are, in fact, made to the universal standard of 40 per cent alcohol by volume. Mescal, the similar spirit which has earned notoriety from the producers' custom of including a pickled worm in each bottle, can be substituted for tequila in all the following recipes.

## Acapulco

- ▮ tequila
- ▮ white rum
- ▮ freshly squeezed lime juice
- ▮▮▮▮ pineapple juice

*Shake over ice. Strain into ice-filled glasses.*

## Acapulco Gold

- ▮ golden (anejo) tequila
- ▮ golden rum
- ▮ coconut cream
- ▮ grapefruit juice
- ▮▮ pineapple juice.

*Shake over ice. Strain into ice-filled glasses.*

---

Candy is dandy, but liquor is quicker.　　　　　Ogden Nash

## Alamo

- ▪▪ tequila
- ▪ orange juice
- ▪ pineapple juice

*Stir together in an ice-filled tall glass.*

## Bird of Paradise

- ▪▪▪ tequila
- ▪ crème de cacao
- ▪ Galliano
- ▪▪ orange juice
- ▪ fresh cream

*Shake over ice. Strain into wine glasses.*

## Blinding Sunrise

- ▪ tequila
- ▪ vodka
- teaspoon triple sec
- ▪▪▪ orange juice
- 2 dashes grenadine

*Shake all but the grenadine over ice. Strain into a tall, ice-filled glass. Add grenadine and an orange slice.*

*A reinforced variation on the popular Tequila Sunrise theme.*

## Bloody Maria

- ▪ tequila
- ▪▪ tomato juice
- dash lemon juice
- dash Tabasco
- dash Worcestershire sauce

*Shake over ice. Strain into a cocktail glass.*

*A Latin variation of the Bloody Mary.*

## Blue Margarita

- ▪▪▪ tequila
- ▪ blue curaçao
- ▪▪ fresh lime juice

*Shake over ice. Strain into cocktail glasses.*

## Brave Bull

- ▪ tequila
- ▪ Tia Maria

*Stir over ice. Strain into a cocktail glass and add a lemon peel twist.*

## Cactus Rose

- ▮▮ tequila
- ▮ Drambuie
- 2 dashes lemon juice

*Shake over ice. Strain into a cocktail glass.*

## Cara Claudia

- ▮ tequilla
- ▮▮ orange juice

*Shake over ice. Strain into a cocktail glass.*

## Catalina

- ▮▮ tequila
- ▮ peach brandy
- ▮ blue curaçao
- ▮▮ lemon juice
- ▮▮ fresh lime juice

*Shake over ice. Strain into cocktail glasses.*

## Chapala

- ▮▮ tequila
- ▮ equal mix of lemon and orange juice
- dash triple sec
- teaspoon grenadine

*Shake over ice. Strain into a cocktail glass.*

## Coconut Tequila

- ▮ tequila
- 2 dashes coconut liqueur
- 2 dashes lemon juice
- dash maraschino

*Shake over ice. Strain into a cocktail glass.*

---

The ▮ symbol in the recipes is a 'unit' to indicate proportions. A reasonable single measure to use in mixing is about an ounce – equivalent to 30 millilitres (ml). Quantities in the recipes given as dashes, spoonfuls etc., are based on one-ounce unit measures of the accompanying principal ingredients. A cocktail incorporating 2 to 3 measures of alcoholic ingredients makes a reasonably strong drink for one person. Cocktails with 4 or more measures are best made for two or more people.

## El Diablo

▮▮▮ tequila

▮ crème de cassis

▮ fresh lime juice

chilled dry ginger ale

lime peel strips

*Add lime juice and peel to tall, ice-filled glasses. Pour tequila and cassis over.*

## Huatusco Whammer

▮ tequila

▮ rum

▮ vodka

▮ gin

▮ Cointreau

▮▮ lemon juice

teaspoon sugar

Coca-Cola

*Shake all but the Coca-Cola over ice. Strain into ice-filled tall glasses and top with Coca-Cola.*

## Magna Carta

▮▮ tequila

▮ Cointreau

fresh lime juice

chilled sparkling wine

salt

*Prepare small wine glasses by dipping rims in lime juice and then in salt to encrust. Stir spirits of over ice and strain into prepared glasses. Top with sparkling wine.*

## Margarita

▮▮▮ tequila

▮ Cointreau

▮▮ freshly squeezed lime juice

salt

*Prepare cocktail glasses by running lime rind round rim and dipping into salt to encrust. Shake ingredients over ice. Strain.*

*Recipe is attributed to Francisco 'Pancho' Morales (1919–97) who first made the cocktail on 4 July 1942 in Ciudad Juarez, Mexico.*

## Margarita Impériale

- ⚫⚫ tequila
- ⚫⚫ Mandarine Napoléon
- ⚫ freshly squeezed lime juice

dash curaçao

*Prepare cocktail glasses by running lime rind round rim and dipping into salt to encrust. Shake ingredients over ice. Strain.*

## Matador

- ⚫ tequila
- ⚫ fresh lime juice
- ⚫⚫ pineapple juice

*Shake over ice. Strain into an ice-filled cocktail glass.*

## Mexican

- ⚫ tequila
- ⚫ pineapple juice

dash grenadine

*Shake over ice. Strain into a cocktail glass.*

## Mexicola

- ⚫⚫ tequila
- ⚫ fresh lime juice

chilled cola

*Pour tequila and lime into a tall, ice-filled glass. Top with cola and stir to mix.*

## Navajo Trail

- ⚫⚫ tequila
- ⚫ triple sec
- ⚫ fresh lime juice
- ⚫ cranberry juice

*Shake over ice. Strain into cocktail glasses.*

Tequila is distilled from *pulque*, a milky fermented liquor derived from the succulent, cactus-like agave plant. The spirit owes its origins to the first Spanish settlers in Mexico, who did not find *pulque* (a popular tipple among the indigenous population) to their taste, but soon learned that it made an excellent base for distilling.

## Pacific Sunrise

- ⧝ tequila
- ⧝ blue curaçao
- ⧝ fresh lime juice
- dash Angostura bitters

*Shake over ice. Strain into a cocktail glass.*

## Prado

- ⧝⧝⧝ tequila
- ⧝⧝ lemon juice
- ⧝ maraschino
- 4 dashes grenadine
- 1 egg white

*Shake over ice. Strain into cocktail glasses and add maraschino cherries.*

## Rosita

- ⧝⧝⧝ tequila
- ⧝⧝ Campari
- ⧝ dry vermouth
- ⧝ sweet vermouth

*Stir over ice. Strain into cocktail glasses.*

## Shady Lady

- ⧝⧝⧝ tequila
- ⧝ cranberry juice
- ⧝ apple brandy
- 4 dashes fresh lime juice

*Shake over ice. Strain into cocktail glasses.*

## Sloe Teq

- ⧝⧝ tequila
- ⧝ sloe gin
- ⧝ fresh lime juice

*Shake over ice. Strain into ice-filled tumblers.*

## South of the Border

- ⧝⧝ tequila
- ⧝ Tia Maria
- ⧝ fresh lime juice

*Shake over ice. Strain into cocktail glasses.*

## Submarino

❚ tequila

glass of Mexican beer

*Pour measure of tequila into a shot glass and submerge it in the beer.*

*A Mexican concoction to be consumed in moderation, bearing in mind the local slogan: 'Tequeela weel not keel ya, but submareenos weel!'*

## T & T

❚ tequila

chilled tonic water

*Pour tequila into an ice-filled tumbler. Top with tonic and add a lime slice.*

## Tequila Collins

❚❚ tequila

❚ fresh lime juice

teaspoon sugar

chilled sparkling water

*Pour tequila, lime and sugar into a tall, ice-filled glass. Top with sparkling water and stir.*

## Tequila Cooler

❚❚ tequila

❚ fresh lime juice

chilled tonic water

*Shake tequila and lime over ice. Strain into an ice-filled tall glass and top with tonic.*

## Tequila Mockingbird

❚❚ tequila

❚ green crème de menthe

❚ fresh lime juice

*Shake over ice. Strain into cocktail glasses.*

## Tequila Slammer

❚ tequila

❚ lemon juice

chilled sparkling wine

*Mix the tequila and lemon in a tumbler. Top with sparkling wine. Place hand over tumbler to cover, then slam glass on to a bar or table top to mix — then drink in one. Choose a robust glass.*

### Tequila Sour

∎∎ tequila

∎ lemon juice

teaspoon caster sugar

*Shake over ice. Strain into a cocktail glass.*

### Tequila Straight Up

∎ tequila

lime slice

salt

*Pour tequila into a shot glass. Lick the fold of skin between your thumb and index finger and the back of your hand and sprinkle salt on to it. Lick the salt. Suck the lime. Swallow the tequila. Repeat as desired.*

### Tequila Sunrise

∎ tequila

∎∎ orange juice

4 dashes grenadine

*Into an ice-filled tall glass, first pour the tequila, then the orange juice. Stir. Add grenadine.*

### Tijuana Glass

∎∎ tequila

∎ Campari

∎∎ fresh lime juice

*Shake over ice. Strain into cocktail glasses.*

### Toreador

∎∎∎ tequila

∎ crème de cacao

∎ fresh cream

*Shake over ice. Strain into cocktail glasses.*

### Villa Pancho

∎∎ tequila

∎ fresh lime juice

teaspoon sugar

*Shake over ice. Strain into cocktail glasses.*

### Wild Night Out

∎∎∎ tequila

∎∎ cranberry juice

∎ fresh lime juice

soda water

*Shake tequila and juices over ice. Strain into ice-filled tall glasses and add a squirt of soda.*

# VERMOUTH

Many of the cocktails in this book include vermouth. Here are those recipes in which vermouth is the principal ingredient. Vermouths are wine-based apéritif drinks flavoured with an infinite variety of herbs and other plant materials. Styles range from dry, such as France's pale Noilly Prat, to sweet, such as Italy's reddish-brown Rosso vermouth by Martini & Rossi of Turin.

## Addington

- dry vermouth
- sweet vermouth

  soda water

*Stir vermouth over ice. Strain into a tall, ice-filled glass. Top with soda water. Add orange twist.*

## Alice Mine

- sweet vermouth
- kümmel
- Scotch whisky

*Stir over ice. Strain into a cocktail glass.*

## Barracas

- sweet vermouth
- Fernet Branca

*Stir over ice. Strain into a cocktail glass.*

## Cherry Mixture

- dry vermouth
- sweet vermouth

  dash Angostura bitters

  dash maraschino

*Stir over ice. Strain into a cocktail glass and add a maraschino cherry.*

## Chrysanthemum

▮▮ dry vermouth

▮ Bénédictine

3 dashes pastis

*Stir over ice. Strain into a cocktail glass and add orange peel.*

## Combo

▮▮ dry vermouth

4 dashes brandy

2 dashes curaçao

dash Angostura bitters

pinch of sugar

*Shake over ice. Strain into a cocktail glass.*

## Country Club Cooler

▮▮ dry vermouth

teaspoon grenadine

soda water

*Stir in an ice-filled tumbler and top with soda.*

## Crystal Bronx

▮ dry vermouth

▮ sweet vermouth

▮ orange juice

soda water

*Shake over ice. Strain into an ice-filled glass and top with soda.*

## Davis

▮▮ dry vermouth

▮ rum

▮ fresh lime juice

2 dashes grenadine

*Shake over ice. Strain into cocktail glasses.*

## Diplomat

▮▮ dry vermouth

▮ sweet vermouth

dash maraschino

*Stir over ice. Strain into a cocktail glass. Add a maraschino cherry and a lemon slice.*

## Fourth Degree

- ▮▮ dry vermouth
- ▮▮ sweet vermouth
- ▮▮ dry gin
- ▮ pastis

*Stir over ice. Strain into cocktail glasses.*

## Green Room

- ▮▮ dry vermouth
- ▮ brandy
- 2 dashes curaçao

*Stir over ice. Strain into a cocktail glass.*

## John Wood

- ▮▮▮▮ sweet vermouth
- ▮ Irish whiskey
- ▮▮ lemon juice
- ▮ kümmel
- dash Angostura bitters

*Shake over ice. Strain into cocktail glasses.*

## Lusitania

- ▮▮ dry vermouth
- ▮ brandy
- dash orange bitters
- dash pastis

*Stir over ice. Strain into a cocktail glass and sink.*

English farmer Jeremy Hirst (d.1829) was most notorious for his curious attire. He wore bright yellow boots, red-and-white striped breeches, a duck-feather waistcoat and an otter-skin jacket – all crowned with a lambskin hat more than eight feet across. He kept a pack of hunting pigs and had an unrivalled collection of coffins, one of which he used as a drinks cabinet.

## Nineteen

▮▮▮▮ dry vermouth

▮ dry gin

▮ kirsch

dash pastis

teaspoon sugar

*Stir over ice. Strain into cocktail glasses.*

## North Pole

▮▮▮ dry vermouth

▮ pineapple juice

sugar

*Dip rim of cocktail glass into pineapple juice, then into sugar to encrust. Shake vermouth and juice over ice. Strain.*

## Rolls-Royce 3

▮▮ vermouth

▮ dry gin

▮ whisky

dash orange bitters

*Stir over ice. Strain into a cocktail glass.*

*As described by H. E. Bates in The Darling Buds of May, 1958.*

## Roma

▮▮ dry vermouth

▮▮ sweet vermouth

▮ Campari

▮ dry gin

dash Strega

*Stir over ice. Strain into cocktail glasses.*

## Soul Kiss

▮▮ dry vermouth

▮▮ sweet vermouth

▮ Dubonnet

▮ orange juice

*Shake over ice. Strain into cocktail glasses.*

## Trocadero

▮ dry vermouth

▮ sweet vermouth

dash grenadine

dash orange bitters

*Shake over ice. Strain into a cocktail glass and add a maraschino cherry.*

## Velocity

▪▪ sweet vermouth

▪ dry gin

slice orange

*Shake over ice. Strain into a cocktail glass.*

## Vermouth Cocktail

▪ dry or sweet vermouth

dash Angostura bitters

*Stir over ice. Strain into a cocktail glass and add a maraschino cherry.*

## Vermouth & Cassis

▪▪ dry vermouth

▪ crème de cassis

soda water

*Pour vermouth and cassis into an ice-filled tumbler. Top with soda.*

## Vermouth & Curaçao

▪ dry vermouth

teaspoon curaçao

soda water

*Pour vermouth and curaçao into an ice-filled tumbler. Top with soda.*

## Washington

▪▪ dry vermouth

▪ brandy

2 dashes Angostura bitters

2 dashes sugar syrup

*Shake over ice. Strain into a cocktail glass.*

---

Vermouth, named after Anglo-Saxon *vermod* (the shrub wormwood), can claim to be the first western medicine – as made from infusions of herbs in wine by Greek physician Hippocrates (460–359 BC). Apart from wormwood, some fifty flavourings are typically used in vermouths today. They include allspice, camomile, cloves, coriander, forget-me-not, gentian, ginger, hyssop, juniper, quinine and rose petals.

## Whisper

- dry vermouth
- sweet vermouth
- whisky

*Stir over ice. Strain into a cocktail glass.*

## Wyoming Swing

- dry vermouth
- sweet vermouth
- orange juice

sprinkle of sugar

soda water

*Shake vermouth, juice and sugar over ice. Strain into tumblers and top with soda.*

## X-Ray

- Noilly Prat
- dry gin
- white rum

*Stir over ice. Strain into a cocktail glass and add a cocktail olive.*

## York Special

- dry vermouth
- maraschino

2 dashes orange bitters

*Stir over ice. Strain into a cocktail glass.*

## Zanzibar

- dry vermouth
- dry gin
- lemon juice

2 teaspoons sugar syrup

*Shake over ice. Strain into cocktail glasses and add a lemon-peel twist.*

# VODKA

Russia's national spirit has sustained its dedicated drinkers through centuries of hardship, blurring the sharp edges of social, political and climatic privation. The very name betrays what a staple the spirit is in everyday life – it means 'little water'. Commercial vodka is distilled from cereals, mainly rye, and filtered through charcoal to enhance its trademark purity. For mixing purposes, choose standard-strength (around 40 degrees by volume), unflavoured vodkas. Polish and Swedish vodkas should not be overlooked – and do have an ethnicity lacked by most 'Russian' brands, which are commonly produced under licence, far from their country of origin.

## ABM

- **∐** Absolut vodka
- **∐ ∐** tomato juice
- dash Tabasco

*Shake over ice. Strain into an ice-filled tumbler.*

*The initials, so the story goes, stand for Absolutely Bloody Marvellous.*

## Absolute Peach

- **∐** Absolut vodka
- **∐** peach schnapps

*Stir over ice. Strain into a shot glass.*

## Alfie

- **∐ ∐** lemon vodka
- **∐** pineapple juice
- dash Cointreau

*Shake over ice. Strain into a cocktail glass.*

## Apple Day

- vodka
- apple brandy
- apple juice

teaspoon lemon juice

*Shake over ice. Strain into cocktail glasses.*

## Aqueduct

- ∎∎ vodka
- fresh lime juice

2 dashes apricot brandy

2 dashes curaçao

*Shake over ice. Strain into a cocktail glass.*

## Ask Mama

- ∎∎ vodka
- Cointreau
- fresh lime juice

*Stir over ice. Strain into a cocktail glass.*

## Balalaika

- ∎∎ vodka
- Cointreau
- lemon juice

*Shake over ice. Strain into a cocktail glass.*

## Barbie White

- ∎∎ vodka
- Cointreau
- fresh cream

*Shake over ice. Strain into a cocktail glass.*

## Bellinitini

- ∎∎ vodka
- peach schnapps
- fresh peach juice juice

chilled sparkling wine

*Shake spirits and juice over ice. Strain into small wine glasses and top with sparkling wine.*

## Black Magic

- ▮▮ vodka
- ▮ Tia Maria
- dash lemon juice

*Shake over ice. Strain into cocktail glasses.*

## Black Russian

- ▮▮ vodka
- ▮ Kahlúa

*Stir over ice. Strain into a cocktail glass.*

## Bloody Mary

- ▮ vodka
- ▮▮▮ tomato juice
- 2-4 dashes Worcester sauce
- 2-4 dashes lemon juice
- pinch celery salt
- pinch cayenne pepper or dash of Tabasco

*Mix with a spoon in an ice-filled tall glass.*

*There are countless variations of this cocktail, which is said to have been devised during the 1920s by Fernard Petiot of Harry's New York Bar (est. 1911) in Paris.*

---

**Bloody January** is a non-alcoholic edition of the Bloody Mary, alleged to deliver some of the pleasure of the real thing, but with dissimilar effects.

Use a 'juicer' (a type of electrical kitchen device) or food mixer, or mash the ingredients with a fork and press through a coarse sieve.

> 2 large ripe tomatoes, peeled* and quartered
> 1 medium-sized red pepper, quartered and cored
> 1 green chilli, halved and de-seeded
> juice of one fresh lime

Add all the ingredients to your machine or sieve in sequence before mixing. Chill before serving, and add salt and pepper to taste.

\* to skin tomatoes, plunge them into boiling water, then into cold. This loosens the skin, which can then be simply peeled away in your fingers.

## Blue Lagoon

⚍ vodka

3 dashes blue curaçao

chilled clear grape juice

*Combine vodka and curaçao in an ice-filled tall glass. Top with grape juice and stir.*

## Bolshoi

⚍⚍ vodka

⚏ Campari

*Stir over ice. Strain into a cocktail glass and squeeze lemon peel over.*

## Bonzai Fluff

⚍ vodka

⚍ peach schnapps

*Stir over ice. Strain into a cocktail glass.*

## Bullfrog

⚍ vodka

2 dashes Cointreau

lemonade

*Combine spirits in a tall, ice-filled glass. Top with lemonade and add a lemon slice.*

## Bullshot

⚍ vodka

⚏⚏⚏ undiluted canned beef consommé

2 dashes Worcester sauce

2 dashes lemon juice

dash Tabasco

pinch of salt

pinch of cayenne pepper

*Mix with a spoon in an ice-filled tall glass.*

## Cape Cod

⚍ vodka

⚍ cranberry juice

2 dashes fresh lime juice

*Shake over ice. Strain into a cocktail glass.*

## Casablanca

⚍⚍ vodka

⚍ advocaat

teaspoon Galliano

⚍ equal mix lemon and orange juice

*Shake over ice and strain into a tall, ice-filled tumbler.*

## Castle Cary

- ⚫ vodka
- ⚫ sloe gin

*Stir over ice. Strain into a shot glass.*

## Chilli Willy

- ⚫⚫ vodka
- teaspoon of freshly chopped hot chilli

*Shake over ice. Strain into cocktail glasses.*

*The 'temperature' of this interesting cocktail is controlled according to the amount of chilli incorporated and whether the seeds (by far the hottest component) are included. Only for the brave (or foolhardy).*

## Citronella

- ⚫ lemon vodka
- ⚫ cranberry juice
- 2 dashes lime juice

*Shake over ice and strain into a cocktail glass.*

## Clapham Omnibus

- ⚫⚫ Absolut vodka
- ⚫ Campari
- ⚫ sweet vermouth

*Stir over ice. Strain into cocktail glasses.*

## Cordless Screwdriver

- ⚫⚫ chilled vodka
- an orange wedge dipped in sugar

*Pour the vodka into a shot glass. Drink the vodka in one shot, and take a good suck of the orange.*

## Cosmo

- ⚫⚫ vodka
- ⚫ Cointreau
- ⚫⚫ cranberry juice
- ⚫ fresh lime juice

*Shake over ice. Strain into cocktail glasses and squeeze lemon peel over.*

---

I thought Honking was a town in China until I discovered Smirnoff.
1970s parody of a celebrated advertising campaign

## Cosmos

**❚❚❚** vodka

**❚** fresh lime juice

*Shake over ice. Strain into shot glasses.*

## Cossack

**❚** vodka

**❚** cognac

**❚** fresh lime juice

sprinkling of sugar

*Shake over ice. Strain into a cocktail glass.*

## Crocodile

**❚❚** vodka

**❚** melon liqueur

**❚** Cointreau

**❚❚** lemon juice

*Shake over ice. Strain into cocktail glasses.*

## Czarina

**❚❚❚❚** vodka

**❚** dry vermouth

**❚** apricot brandy

dash Angostura bitters

*Stir over ice. Strain into cocktail glasses.*

---

The ❚ symbol in the recipes is a 'unit' to indicate proportions. A reasonable single measure to use in mixing is about an ounce – equivalent to 30 millilitres (ml). Quantities in the recipes given as dashes, spoonfuls etc., are based on one-ounce unit measures of the accompanying principal ingredients. A cocktail incorporating 2 to 3 measures of alcoholic ingredients makes a reasonably strong drink for one person. Cocktails with 4 or more measures are best made for two or more people.

## Downside House

- vodka
- green crème de menthe
- fresh lime juice

*Shake over ice. Strain into a cocktail glass.*

## East Wind

- vodka
- dry vermouth
- sweet vermouth
- 2 dashes rum

*Stir over ice. Strain into cocktail glasses.*

## Edwardian

- vodka
- Dubonnet
- 2 dashes fresh lime juice
- 2 dashes grenadine

*Shake over ice. Strain into a cocktail glass.*

## Electric Jam

- Absolut vodka
- blue curaçao
- mixed lemon and orange juice

*Pour into a tall, ice-filled glass. Stir gently.*

## Fruitini

- vodka
- fruit juice
- teaspoon sugar

*Shake over ice and strain into a cocktail glass.*

*The Fruitini is a popular new genus of cocktails. Make the drink with any fresh fruit juice you like, or, better, make it with juice extracted from fruit by simply pushing it through a sieve. Soft fruits such as raspberries, strawberries and cranberries are particularly suitable, and pineapple is also very much in vogue.*

## Full Monty

- ✚ vodka
- ✚ Galliano
- a sprinkle of grated ginseng root

*Shake over ice. Strain into cocktail glasses.*

## Galactica

- ✚ vodka
- ✚ blue curaçao
- ✚ fresh lime juice
- teaspoon crème de cassis

*Shake over ice. Strain into a cocktail glass.*

## Godmother

- ✚✚ vodka
- ✚ amaretto

*Stir over ice. Strain into a cocktail glass.*

## Gorby

- ✚✚ vodka
- ✚✚ apple juice
- 2 dashes grenadine

*Shake over ice. Strain into cocktail glasses.*

## Gorgeous

- ✚✚ vodka
- ✚ cranberry juice
- ✚ equal mix lemon and orange juice

*Shake over ice. Strain into tumblers filled with crushed ice.*

## Grasshopper 2

- ✚✚ vodka
- ✚ white crème de menthe
- ✚ green crème de menthe

*Stir over ice. Strain into cocktail glasses.*

---

The world's most famous vodka brand, Smirnoff, has been distilled in the United States since 1934 and in Britain since 1952. Only the premium Black Label spirit is exclusively distilled in Moscow. The original Smirnoff vodka came from Poland.

## Grimace & Grin

1 bottle chilled vodka, three-quarters full

handful of sour-flavoured jelly beans

*Melt all but a few of the jelly beans by microwaving them with a little vodka. Add to bottle, along with the remaining intact beans. Seal bottle and shake vigorously before serving in cocktail glasses.*

## Gypsy Rose

⚫⚫ vodka

⚫ Bénédictine

3 dashes grenadine

*Stir over ice. Strain into a cocktail glass.*

## Hair Raiser

⚫⚫ vodka

⚫ Dubonnet

⚫ lemon juice

*Shake over ice. Strain into a cocktail glass.*

## Harvey Wallbanger

⚫ vodka

⚫⚫ fresh orange juice

Galliano

*Shake over ice and strain into an ice-filled tumbler. Top with Galliano to taste.*

*Name is said to derive from that of a southern Californian surfer called Harvey whose thirst for this concoction left him unsteady on his feet in cocktail bars.*

## Hollywood Boulevard

⚫ vodka

⚫⚫ orange juice

chilled dry white wine

mint sprig

*Shake vodka and orange and strain into an ice-filled wine glass. Top with wine and add mint sprig and an orange slice.*

## Huntsman

⚫⚫ vodka

⚫ rum

⚫ fresh lime juice

sprinkling of sugar

*Shake over ice. Strain into cocktail glasses.*

## Jamora

- ▌▌ vodka
- ▌ orange juice
- ▌ apple juice

teaspoon raspberry liqueur

two fresh raspberries per glass (if available)

chilled sparkling wine

*Shake vodka, fruit juices and raspberry liqueur over ice and strain into wine glasses. Add raspberries and top with sparkling wine.*

## Jericho

- ▌▌ vodka
- ▌ blue curaçao
- ▌ lemon juice
- ▌ orange juice

*Shake over ice. Strain into cocktail glasses.*

## Kamikaze

- ▌ vodka
- ▌ Cointreau
- ▌ Rose's Lime Juice cordial

*Shake over ice. Strain into a shot glass.*

## Kangaroo

- ▌▌ vodka
- ▌ dry vermouth

*Stir over ice. Strain into a cocktail glass and squeeze lemon peel over.*

## Kretchma

- ▌▌ vodka
- ▌▌ crème de cacao
- ▌ lemon juice

dash grenadine

*Shake over ice. Strain into cocktail glasses.*

---

Vodka has been one of the great successes of the American drinks industry. In 1950, sales of the spirit in the United States were 386,000 gallons. By 1980, the market had grown by 250 times – to 100 million gallons.

## Kuch Behar

- ▮ pepper vodka
- ▮ tomato juice

*Pour into an ice-filled tumbler and stir.*

*A variation on the Bloody Mary said to have been devised by the ruler of the eponymous Indian province.*

## La Stupenda

- ▮▮ vodka
- ▮ fresh cream
- ▮ raspberry liqueur

*Shake over ice. Strain into cocktail glasses.*

*Allegedly named in honour of Australia's great soprano, Dame Joan Sutherland.*

## Long Island Tea

- ▮▮▮ vodka
- dash of cola

*Stir in an ice-filled long glass.*

*Named after the preferred tipple of New York State denizens who wish to give the right impression to respectable or temperance visitors. The cola is strictly for colouring. Any white spirit will do for this furtive cocktail.*

## Long Slow Comfortable Screw

- ▮ vodka
- ▮ Southern Comfort
- ▮▮ orange juice

*Shake over ice. Strain into an ice-filled tumbler and add orange slice.*

*An indelicately titled variation on the Screwdriver.*

## Louisa

- ▮ vodka
- ▮▮ tomato juice
- teaspoon lemon juice
- 4 dashes Worcestershire sauce
- pinch of freshly ground black pepper
- chilled sparkling water

*Stir all except sparkling water over ice in tall tumblers. Top with sparkling water and add cocktail olives.*

## Mars Attacks

1 bottle vodka

6 Mars Bars

*Chop Mars Bars into small pieces and place in a heatproof dish. Add a slug of vodka. Place in a microwave oven and cook for 30 seconds. Remove, and stir in the rest of the vodka until the mix is liquid. Transfer to a jug, refrigerate and serve when cold.*

*The author thanks Sidwell Coe for this curious recipe, and freely confesses to having chickened out of testing it. Mixers are advised to proceed with caution.*

## Melon State Balls

⚈ vodka

⚈ melon liqueur

⚈ orange juice

*Shake over ice. Strain into cocktail glasses.*

## Molotov

⚈ vodka

⚈ Sambuca

*Stir over ice and strain into a liqueur or sherry glass. Add a maraschino cherry.*

The incendiary Molotov Cocktail commemorates Vyacheslav Mikhailovich Skriabin, the Russian known by his fellow revolutionaries as Molotov, 'the Hammer'. The eponymous petrol bomb was neither invented nor employed by Molotov. It was first used as a weapon by Finnish resistance fighters in 1940 – against Russian tanks. Molotov's actual achievements included the division of post-war Germany and the dangerous exacerbation of the Cold War. Expelled by Khrushchev from the Communist party in 1957 as 'a saboteur of peace' and sent to Outer Mongolia, this persistent man nevertheless survived to be reinstated as a party member in 1984, aged 93.

## Monday Blues

∎ vodka

teaspoon blue curaçao

teaspoon Cointreau

*Stir over ice. Strain into cocktail glasses and squeeze lemon peel over.*

## Moon Landing

∎ vodka

∎ amaretto

∎ Baileys Irish Cream

∎ Tia Maria

*Shake over ice. Strain into shot glasses.*

## Moscow Mule

∎∎ vodka

∎ fresh lime juice

chilled ginger beer

*Shake vodka and lime over ice. Strain into an ice-filled tumbler and top with ginger beer. Add lime slice.*

## Ninotchka

∎∎∎ vodka

∎ crème de cacao

∎ lemon juice

*Shake over ice. Strain into cocktail glasses.*

---

It is a popular myth that vodka was originally distilled from potatoes. The first versions of the drink, made in Poland and Russia from the twelfth century, were from grain, and known as 'bread wine'. Production standards improved noticeably when Tsar Peter the Great (1672–1725) devised an improved vodka still. Today, vodka tends to be made from the most available local material. Thus, while Polish and western-Russian versions are still grain-based, Byelrussia tends to potatoes and Ukraine to molasses.

## Olly's

- ▓▓ vodka
- ▓▓ Cointreau
- ▓▓ cava (or other sparkling wine)
- ▓ lemon juice
- small scoop vanilla ice cream

*Shake with ice (or whizz with ice in a liquidiser) and serve in chilled, frosted wine glasses.*

## Peach Buck

- ▓▓▓ vodka
- ▓ peach brandy
- ▓ lemon juice
- chilled dry ginger ale

*Shake spirits and lime over ice. Strain into ice-filled tall glasses and top with ginger ale.*

## Porte Cochère

- ▓▓▓ vodka
- ▓ apricot brandy
- ▓ orange juice
- teaspoon grenadine
- 1 egg yolk

*Shake over ice. Strain into cocktail glasses.*

## Priam's Daughter

- ▓▓ vodka
- ▓ cherry brandy
- dash orange bitters

*Stir over ice. Strain into a cocktail glass.*

## Purple Haze

- ▓ vodka
- ▓ grape juice
- ▓ grapefruit juice
- teaspoon sugar

*Shake over ice. Strain into an ice-filled tumbler.*

## Road Runner

- **⫶⫶** vodka
- **⫶** amaretto
- **⫶** coconut liqueur

*Shake over ice. Strain into cocktail glasses.*

## Russian

- **⫶** vodka
- **⫶** dry gin
- **⫶** crème de cacao

*Stir over ice. Strain into a cocktail glass.*

## Screwdriver

- **⫶** vodka
- **⫶⫶** orange juice

*Stir over ice. Strain into an ice-filled tumbler and add an orange slice.*

## Seabreeze

- **⫶** Absolut vodka
- **⫶⫶** cranberry juice
- **⫶⫶** grapefruit juice

*Shake over ice. Strain into tall ice-filled glasses.*

## Sex on the Beach

- **⫶⫶** vodka
- **⫶** peach brandy
- **⫶⫶** cranberry juice
- **⫶** equal mix of orange and pineapple juice

*Shake over ice. Strain into shot glasses and add a maraschino cherry to each.*

---

Sergei Vasilevich Rachmaninov's First Symphony (in D minor) had its début performance in St Petersburg in 1897, when the Russian composer was just twenty-four years old. But the conductor, Glazunov, was very drunk and made a hash of it. The orchestra was booed off the stage. The symphony did not get another performance until 1945 – two years after Rachmaninov's death at the age of seventy.

## Siberian Sunrise

- ▮ vodka
- ▮ orange juice
- ▮ pineapple juice
- 2 dashes grenadine

*Pour vodka and juices over ice in a tall glass. Add grenadine.*

## Silver Arrow

- ▮▮▮ vodka
- ▮ crème de cassis
- ▮ fresh cream

*Shake over ice. Strain into cocktail glasses.*

## Stockholm

- ▮▮ Absolut lemon vodka
- ▮ lemon juice
- sugar lump
- chilled sparkling wine

*Place sugar lump in a wine glass and add vodka and lemon juice. Stir to dissolve sugar. Top with sparkling wine.*

## Tovaric

- ▮▮▮ vodka
- ▮▮ kümmel
- ▮ fresh lime juice

*Shake over ice. Strain into cocktail glasses.*

*The name recalls an era wistfully remembered by former members of the Soviet Communist Party. It means 'comrade'.*

## Twister

- ▮▮ vodka
- ▮ fresh lime juice
- chilled tonic water

*Shake vodka and lime over ice. Strain into an ice-filled tumbler and top with tonic.*

## Vodga

- ▮▮▮ vodka
- ▮▮ Strega
- ▮ orange juice

*Shake over ice. Strain into cocktail glasses.*

## Vodka-Cranberry Punch

1 bottle vodka

2 pints (1 litre) cranberry juice

half pint (0.25 litre) dry red wine

1 orange, sliced

6 medium strawberries, sliced

*Combine in a punch bowl with plenty of ice.*

## Vodka Martini

▮ vodka

teaspoon dry vermouth

*Shake over ice. Strain into a cocktail glass.*

*Device of novelist Ian Fleming.*

## Vodka Poolside

▮▮▮ vodka

▮ lemon juice

dash grenadine

pinch sugar

soda water

*Shake first four ingredients over ice. Strain into an ice-filled tumbler and top up with soda. Add orange slice.*

## Vodkatini

▮ vodka

dash dry vermouth

*Stir over ice. Strain into a cocktail glass and add lemon peel twist.*

## Waterfall

▮ vodka

▮▮ puréed fresh watermelon

*Shake over ice. Strain into a tumbler filled with crushed ice.*

## White Russian

▮▮ vodka

▮ white crème de menthe

*Stir over ice. Strain into a cocktail glass.*

## White Spider

▮ vodka

▮ white crème de menthe

*Stir over ice. Strain into a cocktail glass.*

## White Velvet

- ✴✴✴ vodka
- ✴✴ clear crème de menthe
- ✴ fresh cream

dash orange bitters

*Shake over ice. Strain into cocktail glasses.*

## Yeltsin

- ✴✴✴ vodka
- ✴ dry vermouth
- ✴ medium sherry

*Stir over ice. Strain into cocktail glasses and squeeze lemon peel over.*

---

St Vladimir, the Russian ruler who imposed Christianity on his people in the tenth century, had previously considered Islam as a possible national religion. He summoned Mohammedan representatives to explain their faith, but soon discovered that there would be a problem. 'Drink is the joy of the Russians,' he felt obliged to tell them. 'We cannot live without it.'

# WHISKY

Whisky-based cocktails are distinct according to their countries of origin. This section is accordingly partitioned into four: bourbon, Irish whiskey, rye whiskey (including Canadian), and Scotch. If your cocktail cabinet stretches to just one or two of these, don't be put off a bit of experimental substitution. Rye, for example, is a fair double for bourbon, and vice versa. And Irish whiskey can equally be said to enjoy a mutual interchangeability with Scotch.

## Bourbon

First distilled in 1789 in Bourbon County, Kentucky, bourbon is the distinctive whiskey of the United States, accounting for half of all the whiskey made (and drunk) in America. It is made from a mash that must comprise at least 51 per cent maize (corn).

### Allegheny

- bourbon
- dry vermouth
- 2 dashes crème de cassis
- 2 dashes lemon juice
- dash Angostura bitters

*Shake over ice. Strain into a cocktail glass and squeeze lemon peel over.*

### Americana

- bourbon
- dash Angostura bitters
- sugar lump
- chilled sparkling wine

*Place sugar lump in a champagne glass and add bitters, followed by bourbon. Stir to dissolve sugar, then top with sparkling wine. Add an orange slice.*

## Ashley Wilkes

- ▮▮ bourbon
- ▮ peach brandy
- 4 dashes fresh lime juice
- teaspoon sugar
- 4 mint sprigs

*Crush three of the mint sprigs and put them, with the sugar and lime juice, into a tumbler. Add ice. Pour spirits over and stir. Add fourth mint sprig.*

## Big Bang Punch

- 2 bottles bourbon
- 1 bottle rum
- 1 bottle apple brandy
- 3 pints (1.5 litres) Indian tea, pre-chilled
- 3 pints (1.5 litres) orange juice
- 2 pints (1 litre) lemon juice
- 4 tablespoons sugar

*Combine in a punch bowl and chill. Add ice just before serving.*

## Black Hawk

- ▮ bourbon
- ▮ sloe gin

*Stir over ice. Strain into a cocktail glass and add a maraschino cherry.*

## Blue Grass

- ▮ bourbon
- 4 dashes apricot brandy
- 2 dashes lemon juice
- sprinkling of sugar
- soda water

*Add spirits, lemon and sugar to an ice-filled tall glass. Top with soda and stir.*

## Bombardier

- ▮ bourbon
- ▮▮▮ chilled beef consommé
- dash lemon juice

*Combine in an ice-filled tall glass and stir.*

## Boston Sour

- ✶✶ bourbon
- ✶ lemon juice
- teaspoon sugar
- 1 egg white

*Shake over ice. Strain into cocktail glasses and add a maraschino cherry.*

## Bourbon Cobbler

- ✶✶ bourbon
- 4 dashes lemon juice
- teaspoon sugar
- soda water

*Mix lemon juice and sugar in a tall glass before adding ice cubes and bourbon. Top with soda and stir.*

## Bourbon Daisy

- ✶✶✶ bourbon
- ✶ Southern Comfort
- ✶ lemon juice
- 2 dashes grenadine

*Shake over ice. Strain into cocktail glasses.*

## Brighton

- ✶ bourbon
- ✶ Bénédictine
- ✶ brandy
- ✶ lemon juice
- ✶ orange juice
- soda water

*Shake all but the soda over ice. Strain into tall, ice-filled glasses and top with soda.*

The ✶ symbol in the recipes is a 'unit' to indicate proportions. A reasonable single measure to use in mixing is about an ounce – equivalent to 30 millilitres (ml). Quantities in the recipes given as dashes, spoonfuls etc., are based on one-ounce unit measures of the accompanying principal ingredients. A cocktail incorporating 2 to 3 measures of alcoholic ingredients makes a reasonably strong drink for one person. Cocktails with 4 or more measures are best made for two or more people.

## Colonel Collins

- ❚❚ bourbon
- ❚ lemon juice
- teaspoon sugar
- chilled soda water

*Stir bourbon, lemon and sugar in a tall, ice-filled tumbler. Top with soda and add a lemon slice.*

## Comfortable Blend

- ❚❚ bourbon
- ❚ Southern Comfort
- ❚ equal mix of lemon and peach juice
- 4 dashes dry vermouth
- teaspoon sugar

*Shake over ice. Strain into ice-filled tumblers.*

## Commuter

- ❚❚❚ bourbon
- ❚ sweet vermouth
- ❚ grenadine

*Shake over ice. Strain into cocktail glasses.*

## Earthquake

- ❚ bourbon
- ❚ gin
- ❚ pastis

*Stir over ice. Strain into a cocktail glass.*

## Embassy

- ❚❚ bourbon
- ❚❚ Drambuie
- ❚ sweet vermouth
- 4 dashes orange juice

*Shake over ice. Strain into cocktail glasses.*

## Horse's Neck

- ❚❚ bourbon
- 1 lemon
- chilled dry ginger ale

*Peel the lemon to make a continuous spiral of rind. Suspend this over a tall glass and pack ice in so the peel extends the full height of the glass. Add the bourbon and top with ginger ale. Stir carefully.*

## Imperial Fizz

- ▮▮ bourbon
- ▮ lemon juice
- teaspoon sugar
- soda water

*Shake bourbon, lemon and sugar over ice. Strain into a tall glass and top with soda.*

## Jumping Julep

- ▮▮▮ bourbon
- ▮ crème de menthe
- ▮ fresh lime juice
- teaspoon sugar
- 4 mint sprigs
- soda water

*Shake all the ingredients except two of the mint sprigs and the soda over ice. Strain into wine glasses and add soda and mint sprigs.*

## Kentucky

- ▮▮ bourbon
- ▮ pineapple juice

*Shake over ice. Strain into a cocktail glass.*

## Kentucky Colonel

- ▮▮▮ bourbon
- ▮ Bénédictine

*Stir over ice. Strain into cocktail glasses*

## Ladies

- ▮ bourbon
- 2 dashes Anisette
- 2 dashes pastis
- dash Angostura bitters

*Stir over ice. Strain into a cocktail glass.*

---

The man is killing time – there's nothing else.
   No help now from the fifth of bourbon
chucked helter-skelter into the river.
   Even its cork sucked under.

Robert Lowell, *The Drinker*

## Lieutenant

▪▪ bourbon

▪ apricot brandy

▪ grapefruit juice

teaspoon sugar

*Shake over ice. Strain into cocktail glasses.*

## Loretto Lemonade

▪ Maker's Mark bourbon

▪ Midori

▪▪ apple juice

tablespoon fresh lime juice

chilled ginger beer

*Shake all but ginger beer over ice. Strain into an ice-filled tumbler. Top with ginger beer, stir and garnish with starfruit.*

*Created by Jamie Terrel of Atlantic.*

## Loretto's Lady

▪▪ Maker's Mark bourbon

▪ Cointreau

chilled dry ginger ale

*Stir spirits in a tall, ice-filled glass. Top with ginger ale and add strawberry slices and mint.*

*Created by Gavin Esler.*

## Mint Julep

▪▪ bourbon

teaspoon sugar

mint sprigs

soda water

*Place 4 mint leaves and the sugar in a stemmed glass. Add a dash of soda and stir the mix to release the mint flavour. Pour in the bourbon, add ice and top with soda. Decorate with mint sprigs.*

The American term julep derives, curiously, from Arabic *julab*, meaning rose water.

## Nevins

**⦚⦚⦚** bourbon

**⦚** mixed grapefruit and lemon juice

4 dashes apricot brandy

dash Angostura bitters

*Shake over ice. Strain into cocktail glasses.*

## Night Owl

**⦚** bourbon

4 dashes Cointreau

4 dashes lemon juice

chilled soda water

*Shake all but soda over ice. Strain into an ice-filled tumbler and top with soda.*

## Old Fashioned

**⦚⦚** bourbon

teaspoon water

dash Angostura bitters

sugar lump

*Place sugar lump in a tumbler and add bitters. Add water to dissolve sugar. Add bourbon and stir. Finally, add ice cubes. Garnish with fruit slices if preferred.*

*This is one of the longest-established cocktails, known in the southern United States since the late eighteenth century. It can also be made with rye whiskey.*

---

Mother love, particularly in America, is a highly respected and much pubicised emotion and, when exacerbated by gin and bourbon, it can become extremely formidable.

Noël Coward, *Future Indefinite*

## Old Pale

- ∷ bourbon
- ∷ Campari
- ∷ dry vermouth

*Stir over ice. Strain into a cocktail glass and squeeze lemon peel over.*

## Rittenhouse

- ∷ bourbon
- ∷ crème de cacao
- ∷ fresh cream

*Shake over ice. Strain into cocktail glasses.*

## Trilby

- ∷ bourbon
- ∷ sweet vermouth
- dash orange bitters

*Stir over ice. Strain into a cocktail glass.*

## Twin Peaks

- ∷ bourbon
- ∷ Bénédictine
- ∷ fresh lime juice
- 2 dashes Cointreau

*Shake over ice. Strain into cocktail glasses and add a lime slice to each.*

## Whiskey Cobbler

- ∷ bourbon
- ∷ orange juice
- teaspoon sugar
- chilled sparkling water

*Shake bourbon, orange and sugar over ice. Strain into ice-filled tumblers and top with sparkling water.*

## Whiskey Flip

- ∷ bourbon
- teaspoon sugar
- 1 egg

*Shake over ice. Strain into cocktail glasses.*

# Irish

Distilled principally from malted barley, the whiskey of Ireland is said to be the oldest of all pot-still whiskies. The art of distilling cereals (as distinct from wine) was very probably discovered in Ireland as much as a millennium ago – centuries before it reached Scotland. As a rule, Irish whiskey has a lighter, less peaty and smoky style than Scotch.

## All Ireland

- ▮ Irish whiskey
- 2 dashes green Chartreuse
- dash crème de menthe

*Stir over ice. Strain into a cocktail glass and add a green olive.*

## Blackthorn Bush

- ▮ Irish whiskey
- ▮ dry vermouth
- 2 dashes pastis
- 2 dashes Angostura bitters

*Stir over ice. Strain into a cocktail glass.*

## Blarney Stone

- ▮ Irish whiskey
- 2 dashes white curaçao
- 2 dashes pastis
- dash maraschino

*Stir over ice. Strain into a cocktail glass.*

## Border Rider

- ▮▮ Irish whiskey
- ▮ apple brandy
- teaspoon sloe gin
- chilled sparkling water

*Pour spirits into a tall, ice-filled glass. Top with sparkling water and stir.*

## Brainstorm

▮▮ Irish whiskey

teaspoon dry vermouth

2 dashes Bénédictine

*Stir over ice. Strain into a cocktail glass and add an orange slice.*

## Colleen

▮▮▮ Irish whiskey

▮▮ Irish Mist

▮ Cointreau

teaspoon lemon juice

*Shake over ice. Strain into cocktail glasses.*

## Irish

▮ Irish whiskey

2 dashes curaçao

2 dashes pastis

dash Angostura bitters

dash maraschino

*Stir over ice. Strain into a cocktail glass and add a cocktail olive.*

## Irish Ayes

▮ Irish whiskey

teaspoon green Chartreuse

*Stir over ice. Strain into a cocktail glass.*

---

'Twas an evening in November,
As I very well remember,
I was strolling down the street in drunken pride.
But my knees were all aflutter,
So I landed in the gutter,
And a pig came up and lay down by my side.

Yes, I lay there in the gutter
Thinking thoughts I could not utter,
When a colleen passing by did softly say,
'You can tell a man who boozes
By the company he chooses.'
At that the pig got up and walked away.

Anon

# Irish Coffee

- ⚫ Irish whiskey
- cup of hot black coffee
- warmed double cream
- teaspoon sugar

*Put whiskey, coffee and sugar into a sturdy stemmed glass. Pour cream on top to float on the surface.*

# Irish Cooler

- ⚫⚫ Irish whiskey
- soda water

*Pour whiskey into a tall, ice-filled glass and top with soda. Add lemon-peel twist.*

# Kerry Cooler

- ⚫⚫ Irish whiskey
- ⚫ dry sherry
- ⚫ lemon juice
- 4 dashes Amaretto
- soda water

*Shake all but the soda over ice. Strain into ice-filled tumblers and add soda.*

# Paddy

- ⚫ Irish whiskey
- ⚫ sweet vermouth
- dash Angostura bitters

*Stir over ice. Strain into a cocktail glass.*

# Shamrock

- ⚫ Irish whiskey
- ⚫ dry vermouth
- 3 dashes crème de menthe
- 3 dashes green Chartreuse

*Stir over ice. Strain into a cocktail glass.*

# Shillelah

- ⚫⚫ Irish whiskey
- ⚫ sherry
- teaspoon rum
- teaspoon sloe gin
- teaspoon lemon juice
- pinch caster sugar

*Shake over ice. Strain into a cocktail glass and add a maraschino cherry.*

## Tipperary

- ▌ Irish whiskey
- ▌ sweet vermouth
- ▌ green Chartreuse

*Stir over ice. Strain into a cocktail glass.*

## Wild Irish Rose

- ▌▌▌ Irish whiskey
- ▌ fresh lime juice
- ▌ grenadine
- chilled soda water

*Shake whiskey, lime and grenadine over ice. Strain into tall, ice-filled glasses and top with soda.*

---

The ▌ symbol in the recipes is a 'unit' to indicate proportions. A reasonable single measure to use in mixing is about an ounce – equivalent to 30 millilitres (ml). Quantities in the recipes given as dashes, spoonfuls etc., are based on one-ounce unit measures of the accompanying principal ingredients. A cocktail incorporating 2 to 3 measures of alcoholic ingredients makes a reasonably strong drink for one person. Cocktails with 4 or more measures are best made for two or more people.

# Rye

The original whiskey of the United States, rye is distilled from a mash composed at least half of rye (as opposed to the barley used largely for Scotch). Canadian whiskey (note the different spelling) is often rye-based, too.

## Algonquin

- ▮▮ rye
- ▮ dry vermouth
- ▮ pineapple juice

*Shake over ice. Strain into a sherry or cocktail glass.*

*Recipe of the Algonquin Hotel in New York City, where literary legends (and legendary drinkers) such as Robert Benchley, Dorothy Parker and Alexander Woolcott famously enjoyed this cocktail at their Round Table.*

## Boomerang

- ▮ rye
- ▮ dry vermouth
- ▮ Swedish Punsch
- dash lemon juice
- dash Angostura bitters

*Stir over ice. Strain into a cocktail glass.*

## Brooklyn

- ▮▮ rye
- ▮ dry vermouth
- dash Amer Picon bitters
- dash maraschino

*Stir over ice. Strain into a cocktail glass.*

## Cablegram

▮▮ rye

▮ lemon juice

teaspoon caster sugar

dry ginger ale

*Shake first three ingredients over ice. Strain into a small wine glass. Top up with ginger ale.*

## Canada

▮▮ Canadian rye

4 dashes Cointreau

dash Angostura bitters

*Stir over ice. Strain into a cocktail glass.*

## Canadian Cherry

▮▮▮ Canadian rye

▮ cherry brandy

▮ mixed lemon and orange juice

*Shake over ice. Strain into cocktail glasses.*

## Canadian Whiskey

▮▮ Canadian rye

2 dashes Angostura bitters

2 teaspoons Gomme syrup

*Shake over ice. Strain into a cocktail glass.*

## Capetown

▮ rye

▮ Capéritif

3 dashes cuaçao

dash Angostura bitters

*Stir over ice. Strain into a cocktail glass.*

## Commodore

▮▮ rye

▮ fresh lime juice

dash orange bitters

teaspoon sugar

*Shake over ice. Strain into a cocktail glass.*

## Cowboy

- ▮▮ rye
- ▮ fresh cream

*Shake over ice. Strain into a glass filled with crushed ice.*

## Creole 2

- ▮ rye
- ▮ sweet vermouth
- 2 dashes Bénédictine
- 2 dashes Amer Picon bitters

*Stir over ice. Strain into a cocktail glass.*

## Crow

- ▮ rye
- ▮▮ lemon juice
- dash grenadine

*Shake over ice. Strain into a cocktail glass.*

## Dandy

- ▮ rye
- ▮ Dubonnet
- 3 dashes Cointreau
- dash Angostura bitters

*Stir over ice. Strain into a cocktail glass.*

## Derby Fizz

- ▮▮ rye
- ▮ lemon juice
- 4 dashes curaçao
- 1 egg
- teaspoon sugar
- soda water

*Shake all but the soda over ice. Strain into a tall, ice-filled glass and top with soda.*

## De Rigueur

- ▮▮ rye
- ▮ grapefruit juice
- ▮ clear honey

*Shake over ice. Strain into a cocktail glass.*

## Dinah

- ▮ rye
- ▮ lemon juice
- teaspoon sugar
- 2 fresh mint sprigs

*Shake with one crushed mint sprig over ice. Strain into a cocktail glass. Add other mint sprig, uncrushed, to glass.*

## Eggnog

■■ rye

■■■■ fresh milk

1 egg

teaspoon sugar

sprinkle of nutmeg

*Shake all but nutmeg over ice and strain into wine glasses. Sprinkle nutmeg over.*

*There are infinite variations on the eggnog theme featuring rum and brandy as substitutes for the rye and additions such as cream and liqueurs.*

## Elk 2

■■ rye

■ port

4 dashes lemon juice

1 egg white

teaspoon sugar

*Shake over ice. Strain into cocktail glasses.*

## Fox River

■■■ rye

■ crème de cacao

4 dashes peach bitters

*Place ice cubes into small wine glasses and pour ingredients over.*

## Ginza Fizz

■■■ sherry

■ port

■ lemon juice

1 egg white

teaspoon sugar

soda water

*Shake all but the soda over ice. Strain into tumblers and top with soda.*

---

Brendan Behan, the thirsty Irish playwright, failed to make a London rendezvous with a friend and offered no apology until the two met by chance in Toronto several months later.

'I was on my way to meet you when an advert on the side of a bus caught my eye,' Behan explained. 'It said, "Drink Canada Dry". So I thought I'd come straight over here and see what I could do.'

## Gloom Lifter

■■■■ rye

■■ lemon juice

1 egg white

teaspoon sugar

*Shake over ice. Strain into cocktail glasses.*

## Habitant

■ rye

4 dashes dry vermouth

4 dashes maple syrup

dash Angostura bitters

*Shake over ice. Strain into a cocktail glass.*

## Ink Street

■ rye

■ lemon juice

■ orange juice

*Shake over ice. Strain into a cocktail glass.*

## Jack Frost

■ rye

■ dry sherry

■ port

*Stir in an ice-filled tumbler. Add orange slice.*

## King Cole

■ rye

2 dashes sugar syrup

dash Fernet Branca

*Stir over ice. Strain into a cocktail glass and add slices of orange and pineapple.*

## Ladies 2

■ rye

dash Angostura bitters

dash Anisette

dash pastis

*Stir over ice. Strain into a cocktail glass.*

## Lawhill

▮▮ rye

▮ dry vermouth

2 dashes maraschino

2 dashes pastis

dash Angostura bitters

*Shake over ice. Strain into a cocktail glass.*

## Loose Moose

▮▮ Canadian rye

▮ dry vermouth

dash Angostura bitters

dash maraschino

dash pastis

*Stir over ice. Strain into a cocktail glass.*

## Los Angeles

▮▮▮▮ rye

▮ lemon juice

dash sweet vermouth

4 teaspoons sugar

1 egg

*Shake over ice. Strain into cocktail glasses.*

## Manhasset

▮▮ rye

▮ mixed dry and sweet vermouth

▮ lemon juice

*Shake over ice. Strain into cocktail glasses and squeeze lemon peel over.*

## Manhattan

▮▮ rye

▮ sweet vermouth

dash Angostura bitters

*Stir over ice. Strain into a cocktail glass and add a cocktail cherry.*

*To make a 'Dry' Manhattan substitute dry vermouth for sweet. For a 'Sweet' Manhattan use equal measures of rye and sweet vermouth.*

## Mountain

▮▮▮ rye

▮ dry vermouth

▮ sweet vermouth

▮ lemon juice

1 egg white

*Shake over ice. Strain into cocktail glasses.*

## New York

∎∎ rye

∎ fresh lime juice

dash grenadine

*Shake over ice. Strain into a cocktail glass.*

## New York Sour

∎∎ rye

∎ lemon juice

teaspoon sugar

chilled dry white wine

*Shake all but wine over ice. Strain into wine glasses and top with wine.*

## Old Pal

∎ rye

∎ Campari

∎ dry vermouth

*Stir over ice. Strain into a cocktail glass.*

## Opening

∎∎ rye

∎ sweet vermouth

∎ grenadine

*Stir over ice. Strain into a cocktail glass.*

## Oriental

∎∎ rye

∎ white curaçao

∎ sweet vermouth

∎ fresh lime juice

*Shake over ice. Strain into cocktail glasses.*

## Palmer

∎ rye

dash lemon juice

dash Angostura bitters

*Shake over ice. Strain into a cocktail glass.*

## Rattler

∎∎∎∎ rye

∎ lemon juice

2 dashes pastis

teaspoon sugar

1 egg white

*Shake over ice. Strain into cocktail glasses.*

## Russell House

∎ rye

3 dashes blackberry liqueur

2 dashes orange bitters

2 dashes sugar syrup

*Shake over ice. Strain into a cocktail glass.*

## Rye Whiskey Cocktail

∎ rye

teaspoon sugar

dash Angostura bitters

*Stir over ice. Strain into a cocktail glass and add a maraschino cherry.*

## Sazerac

∎ rye

dash Angostura bitters

sugar lump

dash pastis

*Shake rye, bitters and sugar over ice. Strain into a chilled cocktail glass. Add pastis and squeeze lemon peel over.*

## Scoff-Law

∎ rye

∎ dry vermouth

∎ grenadine

∎ lemon juice

dash orange bitters

*Shake over ice. Strain into a cocktail glass.*

## SG

∎ rye

∎ lemon juice

∎ orange juice

teaspoon grenadine

*Shake over ice. Strain into a cocktail glass.*

## Soul Kiss 2

- ❚ rye
- ❚ dry vermouth
- ❚ Dubonnet
- ❚ orange juice
- slice of orange

*Shake over ice. Strain into cocktail glasses.*

## Temptation

- ❚ rye
- dash curaçao
- dash Dubonnet
- dash pastis
- strip lemon peel
- strip orange peel

*Shake over ice. Strain into a cocktail glass.*

## Three Rivers

- ❚❚❚ Canadian rye
- ❚ Dubonnet
- 3 dashes Cointreau

*Stir over ice. Strain into cocktail glasses.*

## TNT

- ❚ rye
- ❚ pastis

*Stir over ice. Strain into a cocktail glass.*

## Up-to-Date

- ❚ rye
- ❚ dry sherry
- dash Angostura bitters
- dash Grand Marnier

*Stir over ice. Strain into a cocktail glass.*

---

The ❚ symbol in the recipes is a 'unit' to indicate proportions. A reasonable single measure to use in mixing is about an ounce – equivalent to 30 millilitres (ml). Quantities in the recipes given as dashes, spoonfuls etc., are based on one-ounce unit measures of the accompanying principal ingredients. A cocktail incorporating 2 to 3 measures of alcoholic ingredients makes a reasonably strong drink for one person. Cocktails with 4 or more measures are best made for two or more people.

## Ward Eight

■■ rye

■ lemon juice

■ orange juice

teaspoon grenadine

*Shake over ice. Strain into a cocktail glass.*

## Ward Ten

■■ rye

■ lemon juice

4 dashes grenadine

teaspoon sugar

*Shake over ice. Strain into a cocktail glass.*

## Wedding Bells (1)

■■■ rye

■■ Cointreau

■■ Lillet

dash orange bitters

*Stir over ice. Strain into cocktail glasses.*

## Wedding Bells (2)

■■ rye

■■ Lillet

■ curaçao

dash orange bitters

*Shake over ice. Strain into a cocktail glass.*

## Yankee Punch

3 bottles rye

1 bottle rum

8 pints (4 litres) chilled water

8 heaped tablespoons sugar

*Mix all the ingredients in a punch bowl then add a block of ice (prepared by freezing water in an old ice cream container). Float orange slices on top and serve immediately.*

# Scotch

The Scotch for cocktails is whisky blended from a mixture of malt and grain spirits – under brand names such as Bells, Cutty Sark, Dewars and so on. Single malt Scotch whisky – the likes of Ardbeg, Lagavulin and Macallan – are strictly for enjoying mixed with nothing more than a little pure water.

## Affinity

- ⫶ Scotch
- ⫶ dry vermouth
- ⫶ sweet vermouth
- 2 dashes Angostura bitters

*Stir over ice. Strain into a cocktail glass. Squeeze lemon peel over.*

## Antofagasta

- ⫶ Scotch
- ⫶ dry vermouth
- ⫶ curaçao
- 2 dashes lemon juice

*Shake over ice. Strain into a cocktail glass.*

## Artist's Special

- ⫶⫶ Scotch
- ⫶⫶ dry sherry
- ⫶ lemon juice
- ⫶ redcurrant syrup

*Shake over ice. Strain into a cocktail glass.*

## Beadle

- ⫶ Scotch
- ⫶ dry vermouth

*Stir over ice. Strain into a cocktail glass.*

## Beals

- ⚫⚫ Scotch
- ⚫ dry vermouth
- ⚫ sweet vermouth

*Stir over ice. Strain into a cocktail glass.*

## Blood and Sand

- ⚫ Scotch
- ⚫ cherry brandy
- ⚫ sweet vermouth
- ⚫ orange juice

*Shake over ice. Strain into a cocktail glass.*

## Blues

- ⚫ Scotch
- teaspoon green Chartreuse
- teaspoon curaçao
- dash syrup of prunes

*Stir over ice. Strain into cocktail glasses.*

## Bobby Burns

- ⚫⚫ Scotch
- ⚫⚫ sweet vermouth
- ⚫ Bénédictine

*Stir over ice. Strain into cocktail glasses*

## Bonny Scot

- ⚫⚫ Scotch
- ⚫ Drambuie
- ⚫ lemon juice

*Shake over ice. Strain into a cocktail glass.*

## Cameron's Kick

- ⚫⚫ Scotch
- ⚫⚫ Irish whiskey
- ⚫ lemon juice
- ⚫ Orgeat syrup

*Shake over ice. Strain into cocktail glasses.*

## Chauffeur

- Scotch
- dry vermouth
- dry gin
- dash Angostura bitters

*Shake over ice. Strain into a cocktail glass.*

## Churchill

- Scotch
- Cointreau
- sweet vermouth
- fresh lime juice

*Shake over ice. Strain into cocktail glasses.*

*Sir Winston enjoyed this cocktail, and most other drinks besides. He lived to the age of eighty-nine.*

## Delta

- Scotch
- Southern Comfort
- 2 dashes fresh lime juice
- teaspoon sugar

*Shake over ice. Strain into tall, ice-filled glasses and add an orange slice.*

## Douglas

- Scotch
- dry gin
- grenadine
- 3 dashes Angostura bitters

*Stir over ice. Strain into cocktail glasses.*

## Flying Scotsman

- Scotch
- sweet vermouth
- 4 dashes Angostura bitters
- teaspoon sugar

*Stir over ice. Strain into cocktail glasses.*

## Godfather

- Scotch
- amaretto

*Stir over ice. Strain into a cocktail glass.*

## Harry Lauder

- ☱ Scotch
- ☱ sweet vermouth
- 2 dashes grenadine

*Stir over ice. Strain into a cocktail glass.*

## Highball

- ☲ Scotch
- chilled dry ginger ale or soda water

*Pour whisky into a tall, ice-filled glass and top with ginger ale or soda. Add lemon slice if desired.*

*Highball is an American name for a drink based on any kind of whisky, or even other spirits. The name is from the 'highball' glass - a tall, narrow tumbler.*

## Highland Cooler

- ☳ Scotch
- ☱ lemon juice
- 2 dashes Angostura bitters
- teaspoon sugar
- chilled dry ginger ale

*Shake whisky, juice, bitters and sugar over ice. Strain into a tall glass and top with ginger ale.*

## Hole in One

- ☲ Scotch
- ☱ dry vermouth
- 2 dashes lemon juice
- dash orange bitters

*Shake over ice. Strain into a cocktail glass.*

---

Two dachshunds and a giraffe went into a cocktail bar. They all ordered a shot of whisky on the rocks, topped with ginger ale. When it was time to pay, the dachshunds claimed they had no money. The barman looked grim. The giraffe looked resigned, and said: 'Well, I guess the highballs are on me.'

## Hoots Mon

- ⫶⫶ Scotch
- ⫶ Lillet
- ⫶ sweet vermouth

*Stir over ice. Strain into a cocktail glass.*

## Hopscotch

- ⫶⫶ Scotch
- ⫶ sweet vermouth
- 2 dashes sugar syrup
- dash orange bitters

*Shake over ice. Strain into a cocktail glass.*

## Karl K. Kitchen

- ⫶⫶⫶ Scotch
- ⫶ grape juice
- 4 dashes grenadine

*Shake over ice. Strain into a cocktail glass.*

## Lady Macbeth

- ⫶⫶ Scotch
- 4 dashes lemon juice
- 2 dashes amaretto
- 2 dashes curaçao
- teaspoon sugar

*Shake over ice. Strain into a cocktail glass.*

## Lemon Pie

- ⫶ Scotch
- lemonade

*Pour Scotch over ice in a tumbler. Add lemonade to taste.*

## Linstead

- ⫶ Scotch
- ⫶ pineapple juice
- dash pastis

*Shake over ice. Strain into a cocktail glass and squeeze lemon peel over.*

---

'The Blackenwhite with siphon,' said Dick.
   '*Il n'y a plus de Blackenwhite. Nous n'avons que le Johnny Walkair.*'
   '*Ça va.*'

F. Scott Fitzgerald, *Tender is the Night*

## Loch Lomond

**▮▮** Scotch

teaspoon sugar

dash Angostura bitters

*Stir over ice. Strain into a cocktail glass.*

## Mamie Taylor

**▮▮** Scotch

**▮** fresh lime juice

dry ginger ale

*Shake Scotch and lime over ice. Strain into an ice-filled tumbler and top with ginger ale.*

## Miami Beach

**▮** Scotch

**▮** dry vermouth

**▮** grapefruit juice

*Shake over ice. Strain into a cocktail glass.*

## Mickie Walker

**▮▮▮** Scotch

**▮** sweet vermouth

dash grenadine

dash lemon juice

*Shake over ice. Strain into cocktail glasses.*

## Mint Cooler

**▮▮** Scotch

2 dashes crème de menthe

soda water

*Pour Scotch and crème de menthe into an ice-filled tumbler. Top with soda.*

## Modern

**▮▮** Scotch

4 dashes rum

2 dashes pastis

4 dashes lemon juice

dash orange bitters

*Shake over ice. Strain into a cocktail glass.*

## Morning Glory

■ ■ Scotch

■ ■ lemon juice

2 dashes pastis

1 egg white

teaspoon sugar

chilled sparkling water

*Shake all but sparkling water over ice. Strain into tall, ice-filled glasses and top with sparkling water.*

## MQS

■ ■ Scotch

■ Drambuie

■ green Chartreuse

lemon juice

sugar

*Prepare cocktail glasses by dipping rims in lemon juice and then in sugar to encrust. Stir spirits over ice and strain.*

*The initials stand, of course, for Mary, Queen of Scots.*

## Oh, Henry!

■ Scotch

■ Bénédictine

■ dry ginger ale

*Stir over ice. Strain into a cocktail glass.*

## Pink Heather

■ Scotch

■ strawberry liqueur

chilled sparkling wine

*Pour spirits into a champagne glass and top with sparkling wine. Add a fresh strawberry if you can find one.*

## Piscy Bishop

■ ■ Scotch

■ dry vermouth

teaspoon triple sec

teaspoon orange juice

sprinkling caster sugar

*Shake over ice. Strain into a cocktail glass.*

---

This is the business. The fruit, the fragrance, the cleansing finish on the palate to leave your heart happy, your brain clear and your wits sharp.

Oz Clarke on Highland Park, *Daily Telegraph*

## Rob Roy

▮▮ Scotch

▮ sweet vermouth

*Stir over ice. Strain into a cocktail glass.*

## Rusty Nail

▮ Scotch

▮ Drambuie

*Stir over ice. Strain into a cocktail glass.*

## St Andrew's

▮ Scotch

▮ Drambuie

▮ orange juice

*Shake over ice. Strain into a cocktail glass.*

## Scotch Cooler

▮▮ Scotch

teaspoon crème de menthe

chilled soda water

*Pour spirits over ice in a tumbler. Top with soda and stir.*

## Scotch Kilt

▮▮ Scotch

▮ Drambuie

2 dashes orange bitters

strip orange peel

*Stir over ice. Strain into a cocktail glass.*

## Scotch Mist

▮▮ Scotch

*Shake over ice. Strain into a small wine glass filled with crushed ice. Serve with short straws.*

## Scotch Weekend Sour

▮▮▮ Scotch

▮▮ cherry brandy

▮ sweet vermouth

▮▮ lemon juice

1 egg white

*Shake over ice. Strain into ice-filled tumblers.*

## Shoot

- Scotch
- dry sherry
- mixed lemon and orange juice

sprinkling of sugar

*Shake over ice. Strain into a cocktail glass.*

## Stone Fence

- Scotch

dash Angostura bitters

soda water

*Pour Scotch and bitters into a tumbler containing an ice cube. Top with soda.*

## Strong & Silent

- Scotch
- Cointreau
- lemon juice

*Shake over ice. Strain into a cocktail glass.*

## Sure Shot

- Scotch
- fresh lime juice

2 dashes Angostura bitters

chilled soda water

*Stir Scotch, lime and bitters in an ice-filled tumbler. Top with soda.*

## Thistle

- Scotch
- sweet vermouth

dash Angostura bitters

*Shake over ice. Strain into a cocktail glass.*

## Thunderclap

- Scotch
- brandy
- dry gin

*Stir over ice. Strain into a cocktail glass.*

---

I thought it preferable to any English malt brandy. It was strong, but not pungent, and was free from the empyreumatick taste or smell.
Dr Samuel Johnson on the single occasion
when he drank Scotch whisky

278 *The Wordsworth Ultimate Cocktail Book*

## Toddy

- Scotch

sugar lump

*Add whisky and sugar lump to an ice cube in a small tumbler. Stir well.*

*Other spirits can be substituted.*

## Treble Chance

- Scotch
- Cointreau
- dry vermouth

*Stir over ice. Strain into a cocktail glass.*

## Trilby

- Scotch
- sweet vermouth
- Parfait Amour

2 dashes orange bitters

2 dashes pastis

*Shake over ice. Strain into a cocktail glass.*

## Wembley Park

- Scotch
- dry vermouth
- pineapple juice

*Shake over ice. Strain into a cocktail glass.*

---

'After sojourning a week at Lake Bigler, I went to Steamboat Springs, and beside the steam baths I took a lot of the vilest medicines that were ever concocted. They would have cured me, but I had to go back to Virginia City, where, notwithstanding the variety of new remedies I absorbed every day, I managed to aggravate my disease by carelessness and undue exposure. I finally concluded to visit San Francisco, and the first day I got there, a lady at the hotel told me to drink a quart of whisky every twenty-four hours, and a friend up town recommended precisely the same course. Each advised me to take a quart; that made half a gallon. I did it, and still live.'

Mark Twain, *Curing a Cold*

## Whisky Collins

▪▪▪ Scotch

▪ dry vermouth

▪ pineapple juice

*Shake over ice. Strain into cocktail glasses.*

## Whisky Mac

▪▪ Scotch

▪ ginger wine

*Stir over ice. Strain into a cocktail glass.*

## Whisky Sour

▪▪ Scotch

▪ lemon juice

teaspoon sugar

*Shake over ice. Strain into a cocktail glass. According to personal taste, boost the sourness of this classic cocktail by reducing the proportion of lemon juice.*

*Sours can also be made with brandy and clear spirits.*

## Whisky Special

▪▪▪ Scotch

▪▪ dry vermouth

4 dashes orange juice

pinch of nutmeg

*Shake over ice. Strain into cocktail glasses and add an olive.*

## Whizz-Bang

▪▪ Scotch

▪ dry vermouth

2 dashes grenadine

2 dashes orange bitters

2 dashes pastis

*Stir over ice. Strain into a cocktail glass.*

## Woodward

▪▪ Scotch

▪ dry vermouth

3 dashes grapefruit juice

*Shake over ice. Strain into a cocktail glass.*

---

Not for the faint-hearted.

Nick White on Lagavulin in *Ideal Home*

# WINE

For all the improvements in the standards of winemaking worldwide, there are still plenty of bottles that are immeasurably improved by the addition of an extra ingredient or two. Obviously, cheap wines should be used as the base for mixed drinks – but bear in mind that better wine makes for a better concoction. The hearty red wines and well-flavoured dry whites of the 'New World' are more likely to be suitable than those of European origin.

Recipes based on champagne and sparkling wines, port and madeira and sherry appear under their respective headings.

## Aloha Fizz

- ✂ dry white wine
- ✂ pineapple juice
- ✂ soda water
- caster sugar
- extra soda

*In a tall wine glass stir together the measures of pineapple juice and soda with the sugar. Add crushed ice and then the wine. Top up with the extra soda.*

## Hot Springs

- ✂✂✂ chilled dry white wine
- ✂ pineapple juice
- teaspoon grenadine
- dash orange bitters

*Stir briefly with ice and pour into a wine glass.*

---

Vesuvinum is the world's earliest trademark. It was engraved on the wine jars uncovered at Pompeii, buried in AD79 by the eruption of Vesuvius.

## Kir

chilled white wine

teaspoon (or less) crème de cassis

*Put cassis into a wine glass and top with white wine. Traditionally, Bourgogne Aligoté wine is used.*

*The drink commemorates French partisan and mayor of Dijon, Félix Kir.*

## Manhattan Cooler

■■ dry red wine

teaspoon lemon or lime juice

dash rum

pinch of sugar

*Stir over ice. Strain into a wine glass and add fruit slices.*

## Mint

■■■■ dry white wine

■ dry gin

teaspoon crème de menthe

sprigs fresh mint

*Pour half the wine into the shaker and add two mint sprigs. Leave for two hours. Add ice, remaining wine, gin and crème de menthe and shake. Strain into wine glasses, adding a mint sprig to each.*

## Moonlight

■■ dry white wine

■■ dry gin

■ grapefruit juice

teaspoon kirsch

*Shake over ice. Strain into small wine glasses.*

Wine comes in at the mouth
And love comes in at the eye.
That's all we shall know for truth
Before we grow old and die.
I lift the glass to my mouth,
I look at you, and I sigh.

W. B. Yeats

## Myr

chilled dry white Loire wine

teaspoon Gabriel Boudier Crème de Myrtilles

*Pour Myrtilles into a wine glass. Top with wine.*

*A variation on the theme of Kir suggested to Robin Yapp, wine merchant of Mere in Wiltshire, England, by Harrison Birtwistle.*

## Myra

▮▮ red wine

▮ dry vermouth

▮ vodka

*Stir over ice. Strain into a cocktail glass.*

## Osborne

▮▮▮ claret or similar red wine

▮ Scotch whisky

*Mix together in a wine glass.*

*Favoured by Queen Victoria, who found claret too weak without reinforcement, and named after Osborne House, the Isle of Wight retreat where she died in 1901.*

## Queen Charlotte

▮▮ dry red wine

▮ grenadine

teaspoon lemon juice

sparkling water

*Combine wine, grenadine and lemon juice in a tall wine glass. Add ice cubes and top with sparkling water. Stir.*

## Soho

▮▮ Chianti

▮ sweet vermouth

▮ grapefruit juice

*Shake over ice. Strain into a cocktail glass.*

## Spritzer

chilled dry white wine

chilled sparkling water

*Combine equal quantities in a wine glass.*

If God forbade drinking, would He have made wine so good?

Cardinal Richelieu

## Syllabub

1 pint (0.5 litre) chilled
dry white wine

1 pint (0.5 litre) chilled
fresh cream

4 heaped tablespoons
sugar

4 tablespoons lemon juice

nutmeg

*Whisk all the ingredients
except the nutmeg in a mixing
bowl until thoroughly blended.
Spoon into wine glasses and
grate nutmeg over.*

## Wineapple Cooler

**¦ ¦** dry white wine

**¦ ¦** apple juice

**¦ ¦** sparkling water

teaspoon caster sugar

extra sparkling water

*Combine the measured
ingredients in tall wine glasses
and add ice. Top with extra
sparkling water.*

## Wine Cobbler

**¦ ¦** dry red wine

**¦** sparkling water

teaspoon sugar

*In a wine glass, mix the sugar
and sparkling water before
adding the wine. Add ice, stir
and put in an orange slice.*

## Xerxes II

**¦ ¦** red wine

**¦** brandy

**¦** port

*Combine in a wine glass.*

---

The late oceanographer Jacques Cousteau once salvaged an
amphora of Greek wine from a Mediterranean wreck dated 230BC.
He drank the contents.

# Wine Punches

## Cold Duck

2 chilled bottles Moselle

1 chilled bottle sparkling wine

juice of 1 lemon

1 lemon, sliced

6 teaspoons sugar

*In a punch bowl with plenty of ice cubes (or, better, one large ice block made by freezing the water in an old ice cream container) mix the lemon juice and sugar together first, then add the wine. Float the lemon slices on top.*

*The recipe is German, and originally known as Kalte Ente.*

## Rhine Wine Punch

4 bottles German white wine

1 bottle sparkling water

1 glass brandy

1 glass maraschino

1 teabag

*Chill all ingredients in advance. Combine in a punch bowl. Remove teabag after ten minutes, then add fruit slices.*

According to the Oxford dictionaries, the term punch for a mixed drink comes from Sanskrit *pañca*, meaning five. This is because the original punch was a drink from five different ingredients.

## Sangria

2 bottles red Spanish wine, chilled

small glass Jerez (Spanish) brandy

1 pint (0.5 litre) sparkling water, chilled

juice of 2 oranges and 2 lemons

1 orange and 1 lemon, sliced

4 tablespoons sugar

*Combine all ingredients except sparkling water in a large jug. Refrigerate for an hour or more. Add ice and sparkling water immediately before serving in wine glasses.*

## Sauternes Punch

2 bottles chilled Sauternes

⚫ curaçao

⚫ Grand Marnier

⚫ maraschino

400 grams (1 lb) sugar

*Combine in a punch bowl, stirring to dissolve sugar. Add ice and fruit slices.*

---

The ⚫ symbol in the recipes is a 'unit' to indicate proportions. A reasonable single measure to use in mixing is about an ounce – equivalent to 30 millilitres (ml). Quantities in the recipes given as dashes, spoonfuls etc., are based on one-ounce unit measures of the accompanying principal ingredients. A cocktail incorporating 2 to 3 measures of alcoholic ingredients makes a reasonably strong drink for one person. Cocktails with 4 or more measures are best made for two or more people.

# A Cocktail Glossary

There are scores of different spirits, liqueurs, wines, bitters, flavouring and sweetening preparations and individual branded drinks mentioned among the recipes. The descriptions in this section give some guidance to the character and flavours of these products. If you have interesting bottles such as Chartreuse, crème de cacao, Galliano or Southern Comfort lurking in your cupboard, you may have been wondering for years just what to make of them. To discover in which cocktails these and many other exotic drinks can be used, see the appropriate entry in this glossary.

**advocaat** Brandy-based liqueur of the Netherlands. Egg yolk, sugar and vanilla are principal ingredients. Leading brands include Bols and Warnink. An ingredient in Snowball (Liqueurs & Apéritifs); Casablanca (Vodka).

**amaretto** Almond-flavoured liqueur of Italy. The original brand, Amaretto di Saronno, dates from 1525 and is based on apricot brandy. An ingredient in Alabama Slammer, Amaretto Coffee, Amaretto Cream, Amaretto Rose, Amaretto Stinger, Bushwhacker, Italiano, Rocky Mountain, Yikes (Liqueurs & Apéritifs); Lounge Lizard, Pink Planter (Rum).

**Amer Picon** Gentian and orange flavoured apéritif bitters. French.

**Angostura bitters** Aromatic rum-based bitters flavoured with herbs and spices. Made in Trinidad since early 19th century. Very widely used in cocktails.

**anis** Star-anis-flavoured liquor of France introduced as a substitute for absinthe after its banning in 1915. Leading brand is Pernod.

**anisette** Aniseed-flavoured (with coriander and other herbs added) liqueur of France. Original and leading brand is Marie Brizard. An ingredient in Absinthe Frappé, Suisse, Which Way (Anis & Pastis); Café de Paris, D'Amour, Snowball, White Knight (Gin); Blanche (Liqueurs & Apéritifs); Shanghai (Rum).

**apple brandy**   Spirit distilled from fermented apple juice (cider).

**applejack**   North American name for apple brandy.

**apricot brandy**   Technically, it should be a spirit or *eau-de-vie* distilled from fermented apricots. Many brands are flavoured liqueurs.

**aquavit**   Herb-flavoured grain or potato spirit of Scandinavia. Most common flavouring is caraway.

**armagnac**   The brandy of Gascony. Said to be more fiery and earthy than the brandy of its great rival to the north, Cognac.

**bagaceira**   The *aguardiente* (grape spirit) of Portugal.

**Baileys Irish Cream**   Sweet chocolate-flavoured liqueur compounded of Irish whiskey and Irish double cream. Introduced 1974 and made by R & A Bailey of Dublin, Ireland. An ingredient of La Jolla (Brandy); Rainbow's End (Fruit Brandies); Banjino, Silver Jubilee (Gin); Banana Slip, B-52, Bushwhacker, Golden Nipple, Irish Charlie, Irish Mint, Nutty Professor, Rattlesnake, Slippery Nipple, Tricolor, Unzip A Banana (Liqueurs & Apéritifs); Moon Landing (Vodka).

**banana liqueur**   May be sold under the name crème de banane. An ingredient in Alcudla (Gin); Banana, Banana Slip, Banshee, Unzip A Banana (Liqueurs & Apéritifs); Banana Cocktail, Banana Rum, Chiquita, Mallorca, Panama Hat (Rum).

**Bénédictine**   Monastic 'elixir' produced in Normandy, France, since 1510. The modern, sweet liqueur is flavoured principally with honey, hyssop, cloves, saffron, balm, cinnamon, nutmeg, angelica, coriander and thyme. An ingredient of B&B, Froupe (Brandy); Champagne Cup (Champagne); Honeymoon, Mule's Hind Leg, Widow's Kiss, Le Chanticleer, Merry Widow, Salutation Spring (Fruit Brandies); Honolulu, Oh, Henry!, Rainbow, Widow's Wish (Liqueurs & Apéritifs); Chrysanthemum (Vermouth); Gypsy Rose (Vodka); Brighton, Kentucky Colonel, Twin Peaks (Whiskey – Bourbon); Brainstorm (Whiskey – Irish); Creole (Whiskey – Rye); Bobby Burns (Whisky – Scotch).

**blackberry liqueur**   See crème de mure.

**brandy**   Technically, a spirit distilled from fermented grapes (wine). In fact, spirit distilled or merely flavoured with any kind of fruit.

**Byrrh**   Wine-based apéritif drink with flavourings including herbs, quinine and Peruvian tree bark. See Byrrh cocktails under Liqueurs & Apéritifs.

**cachaca**   Colourless (unless wood-aged) cane spirit of Brazil. In manufacture, similar to rum, but with a distinctly different, drier flavour. Export brands include Pitú and Sao Francisco.

**calvados**   The apple brandy of Normandy. For mixing, use basic

'Vieux' or 'Réserve' spirits which have been matured for the minimum three years. Apple brandies from other regions of France are sold as *eaux-de-vie* de cidre.

**Campari**  Italian herbal bitters flavoured with quinine and distinctively coloured from cochineal. Made by Davide Campari & Co. An ingredient of Capri (Brandy); After One, Londino, Negroni, Windsor Rose (Gin); Americano, Fanny Hill, Old Pal, Old Trout (Liqueurs & Apéritifs); Rosita, Tijuana Glass (Tequila); Roma (Vermouth); Bolshoi, Clapham Omnibus (Vodka); Old Pale (Whiskey – Bourbon).

**Capéritif**  Wine and spirit based herbal-flavoured apéritif of South Africa. An ingredient of Barney Barnato (Brandy); Biltong Dry, Cabaret, Cape, Gin & Cape, Jaberwock, Modder River, Piccad, Seventh Heaven, Transvaal (Gin); Manyann, Swazi Freeze (Liqueurs & Apéritifs); Bush Ranger, Jo'burg (Rum).

**champagne**  The sparkling wine of the strictly defined Appellation Contrôlée region of France, La Champagne. For mixing, use non-vintage brands.

**Chartreuse**  Liqueur of the monastery of La Grand Chartreuse at Grenoble, France. Reputedly flavoured with more than 100 different macerated herbs and made to two strengths, labelled 75 degrees proof (yellow) and 96 degrees proof (green). An ingredient of Champs-Elysées, Chartreuse Daisy, Fourscore (Brandy); Widow's Kiss (Fruit Brandies); Alaska, Bijou, Biter, Green Lady, Jewel, Sand Martin, Spring Feeling, Tailspin, Xantia (Gin); Albertine, Bazooka, Chocolate, Golden Slipper, Jewel, Rainbow, Stars & Stripes, Sunrise, Three Quarter Back, Xantia, Yellow Parrot (Liqueurs & Apéritifs); Choc Shock (Port & Madeira); Irish Ayes (Whiskey – Irish).

**Cherry Heering**  Cherry liqueur produced since 1818 by Peter Heering, Denmark. An ingredient in Queen of Denmark (Liqueurs & Apéritifs).

**cider brandy**  Apple brandy by Somerset Cider Brandy company, England. Use three-year-old for mixing. Five-year-old is a fine digestive drink.

**claret**  The dry red wine of Bordeaux. Use only inexpensive co-operative-produced brands for mixing.

**cobblers**  A group of drinks based on wine or spirits shaken with brandy and/or curaçao.

**coconut liqueur**  Spirit-based drink flavoured with coconut. The best-known of these is Malibu, based on Jamaican rum. An ingredient in Banana Colada, Blue Hawaii, Piña Colada, Pink Planter (Rum); Acapulco Gold, Coconut Tequila (Tequila); Road Runner (Vodka).

**coffee liqueur** Spirit-based drink flavoured with coffee essence. The leading brands are Kahlúa and Tia Maria.

**Cointreau** The world's leading orange liqueur. A colourless 'triple sec' flavoured with a mix of Caribbean bitter-orange peels and sweet Mediterranean oranges, it has been in continuous production at Angers, France, since 1849. Cointreau is an ingredient of many of the cocktails in the Liqueurs & Apéritifs section, and in the following recipes under other headings: Big Boy, Deauville, Newton's Special, Rolls Royce, Sidecar (Brandy); Champagne Cooler, Champagne Sidecar (Champagne); Calvados Cocktail, Margaret Rose, Sutton Place (Fruit brandies); Blue Train, Campden, Cat's Eye, Claridge, Corpse Reviver, Fine & Dandy, Gazebo, Happy Return, Little Devil, Mahjongg, Maiden's Prayer, Montmartre, Orange Bloom, Queen Elizabeth, Sweet Patotie, This Is It, Ulanda, Victor's Special, White Lily (Gin); Banana Daiquiri, Beachcomber, Jade, Kempinski, Limey, Petite Fleur, Sunflower (Rum); Cadiz (Sherry); Huatusco Whammer, Magna Carta, Margarita (Tequila); Balalaika, Barbie White, Cosmo, Kamikaze (Vodka); Churchill (Whisky – Scotch).

**crème de cacao** French chocolate liqueur. Varying sweetnesses and shades from pale to dark chocolate. An ingredient in Brandy Alexander, Dolores, Mikado (Brandy); Fifth Avenue (Fruit Brandies); Alexander, B-52, Poppy, Princess Mary (Gin); Banshee, Grasshopper Surprise, Pink Squirrel, Rattlesnake (Liqueurs & Apéritifs); Chocolate Rum, Golden Gate, Panama (Rum); Bird of Paradise, Toreador (Tequila); Kretchma, Ninotchka, Russian (Vodka); Rittenhouse (Whiskey – Bourbon); Fox River (Whiskey – Rye).

**crème de cassis** Blackcurrant liqueur. Production is centred in Dijon, France. An ingredient in Brandy Cassis (Brandy); Kir Royale (Champagne); Paris, Rose de Chambertin (Gin); Broadway Smile, Byrrh Cassis, Calm Sea, Parisian, Sony & Cher, Stars & Stripes (Liqueurs & Apéritifs); El Diablo (Tequila); Vermouth & Cassis (Vermouth); Silver Arrow (Vodka); Allegheny (Whiskey – Bourbon). Kir (Wine).

**crème de framboise** Raspberry liqueur. An ingredient in Star Daisy (Gin), Framboise (Rum), La Stupenda (Vodka).

**crème de menthe** Mint-flavoured liqueur. Leading brands include green Freezomint by Cusenier. White brands are widely available. An ingredient in Button Hook, Hell, Lady Be Good, Savoy Corpse Reviver, Stinger (Brandy); Ethel (Fruit Brandies); Alexander's Sister, Alexander's Sister-in-Law, Caruso, Monte Carlo Imperial, New Arrival, Playing Fields, White Way, White Wings (Gin); Amaretto Stinger, Crème de Menthe Frappé, Diana,

Grasshopper, Grasshopper Surprise, Irish Charlie, Mocha Mint, Mona Lisa, Tricolor, White Spider (Liqueurs & Apéritifs); Chocolate Rum, Continental, Jade, Miami (Rum); Tequila Mocking Bird (Tequila); White Russian, White Velvet (Vodka); Jumping Julep (Whiskey – Bourbon); Shamrock (Whiskey – Irish); Mint Cooler, Scotch Cooler (Whisky – Scotch); Mint (Wine).

**crème de mûre**    Blackberry/ mulberry liqueur. An ingredient in Polonaise (Brandy); Long Shot, Poop Deck (Liqueurs & Apéritifs); Atlantic (Port & Madeira) Cadiz (Sherry); Russell House (Whiskey – Rye).

**crème de myrtilles**    Bilberry liqueur. An ingredient in Myr (Wine).

**crème de noyaux**    Liqueur from the kernels of apricots and peaches. An ingredient in Mikado (Brandy); Jockey Club, Le Chanticleer, Lily, Old Etonian, Royal Arrival, Silver Bells, Windsor Rose (Gin); Pink Squirrel, Tropical (Liqueurs & Apéritifs); Silver Bells (Rum).

**crème violette**    Liqueur with violet flavouring. An ingredient in Atty, Snowball (Gin); Rainbow, Sunrise (Liqueurs & Apéritifs).

**Crème Yvette**    American branded Parma-violet-flavoured liqueur, with matching colour. An ingredient in Eagle's Dream, New Arrival, Union Jack (Gin); Freedom Fighter, Ping Pong (Liqueurs & Apéritifs).

**curaçao**    Originally, the colourless, orange-flavoured, rum-based liqueur made by Dutch settlers in the Caribbean island of Curaçao. Now, a genus of orange liqueurs of differing styles and colours (eg blue, orange, white) produced in France and the Netherlands. Coloured brands are a very useful addition to any drinks cabinet, as many cocktails depend on colour for much of their appeal. Leading producers include Bols, Cusenier, Dolfi and Marie Brizard.

**Drambuie**    Scotch whisky-based liqueur flavoured with heather and honey. An ingredient in British Festival (Gin); Rusty Nail (Liqueurs & Apéritifs); Mallorca (Rum); Cactus Rose (Tequila); Embassy (Whiskey – Bourbon); Bonny Scot, MQS, St Andrews (Whisky – Scotch).

**'dry' gin**    London or Plymouth gin, as distinct from the sweeter, fuller style of the original gin or genever of the Netherlands.

**Dubonnet**    Wine-based, vermouth-style branded apéritif flavoured with quinine and other ingredients. The recipes in this book are all for the original red version rather than the drier, white 'Blonde' brand. Dubonnet is an ingredient in Phoebe Snow (Brandy); Bentley, Wallaby (Fruit Brandies); Apparent, Appetiser, Aviator, Bartender, Biltong Dry, Jimmy Blanc, Napoleon, Opera, Reverie, Salome, Wedding Bell, Windsor Rose (Gin); Diabola, Dubonnet Fizz, Upstairs, Zaza

(Liqueurs & Apéritifs); Edwardian, Hair Raiser (Vodka); Soul Kiss, Three Rivers (Whiskey – Rye).

*eau-de-vie*    Spirit distilled from fruit. Production is centred in the French region of Alsace.

**egg-nog**    Spirit, milk and egg concoction either home-made or in branded, bottled form.

**Fernet Branca**    Italian bitter-tasting liqueur with both apéritif and digestive properties, as well as alleged powers of remedying hangovers. Produced as Fernet by Martini & Rossi in Turin and by Fratelli Branca in Milan. Best-known brand, however, is French, from Distilleries Fernet-Branca at St Louis, Haut-Rhin. An ingredient in Savoy Corpse Reviver, Stomach Reviver (Brandy); Hanky Panky, Napoleon (Gin); Yodel (Liqueurs & Apéritifs); Barracas (Vermouth); King Cole (Whiskey – Rye).

**fizzes**    A group of drinks based on spirits mixed with lemon juice, sugar and soda water.

**flips**    A group of drinks based on wine or spirits shaken with sugar and egg and traditionally served with a sprinkling of nutmeg.

**Forbidden Fruit**    American brandy-based liqueur brand from shaddock, or pomelo, citrus fruit and additionally flavoured with honey. An ingredient in Beaux Arts and Virgin (Gin).

**fresh lime juice**    Not be confused with lime juice cordial, especially in cocktail mixing.

**Galliano**    Yellow-coloured, honey-and-vanilla-flavoured branded liqueur by Distillerie Riunite of Milan, Italy. An ingredient of After One, Alcudla Sorrento (Gin); Golden Cadillac, Golden Nipple (Liqueurs & Apéritifs); Bossanova, Rum Yellowbird (Rum); Bird of Paradise (Tequila); Casablanca, Full Monty, Harvey Wallbanger (Vodka).

**genever**    The original, full-flavoured gin of the Netherlands.

**gill**    A unit of liquid measure, equivalent to one quarter of a pint.

**gin**    Colourless grain spirit principally flavoured with juniper but also with angelica, aniseed, caraway, coriander and orange peel. London Dry gin and the slightly fuller flavoured Plymouth are both ideal for mixing.

**ginger wine**    Use Stone's Original Green Ginger wine, a wine-based liqueur. An ingredient in Brandy Ginger, Grenadier (Brandy); Byculla (Liqueurs & Apéritifs); Whisky Mac (Whisky – Scotch).

**gomme syrup**    French sweet syrup for cocktail mixing.

**Grand Marnier**    Cognac-based orange liqueur produced at Neauphle le Château, France, since 1827. For mixing, use the basic Cordon Jaune brand. An ingredient of Executive Suite, Iolanthe (Brandy); Sunburst (Fruit Brandies); Leap Year, Lorraine, Marny, Satan's Whiskers, Yellow Daisy (Gin); B-52, Gloom Chaser,

Nutty Professor, Red Lion, St Germain, Tricolor (Liqueurs & Apéritifs); Sauternes Punch (Wine Punches).

**grappa** Italian colourless spirit distilled from the by-products of winemaking. Fiery and alcoholic. An ingredient of Genoa, Grappa/Strega (Liqueurs & Apéritifs).

**grenadine** Non-alcoholic sweet syrup based on pomegranates. Widely used in colouring and flavouring cocktails.

**jigger** Old-fashioned spirit measure equivalent to 1.5 fluid ounces or 45 millilitres.

**julep** A genus of mixed drinks known in the southern United States long before the first mentions of cocktails. Spirit based (usually whisky but sometimes brandy or rum) with ice and/or chilled water and often decorated and flavoured with mint.

**Kahlúa** Mexican coffee liqueur. Produced in Europe by Peter Heering of Denmark. Sweeter than its main rival, Tia Maria. An ingredient in Brown Cow, Kahlúa Cocktail, Rattlesnake (Liqueurs & Apéritifs); Blackout and Torridora (Rum); Black Russian (Vodka).

**kirsch** Cherry *eau-de-vie* of France and Switzerland. An ingredient of Café Kirsch, Charleston, Ostend Fizz, Raffles Knockout, Royal Wedding, Vie en Rose (Liqueurs & Apéritifs).

**kümmel** Caraway-seed-flavoured, colourless liqueur of the Netherlands. An ingredient of

Quelle Vie (Brandy); Green Dragon, Royal Arrival, Silver Streak (Gin); Kingston (Rum); Alice Mine (Vermouth); Tovaric (Vodka).

**Lillet** Wine and armagnac based herbal liqueur by Lillet Frères of Bordeaux, France. An ingredient in Frank Sullivan, Hoopla, Iolanthe, Lilliput, Odd McIntyre (Brandy); Abbey, Bich's Special, Campden, Corpse Reviver, Depth Charge, Eddie Brown, Great Secret, H&H, Jimmy Blanc, Kina, Lily, Lorraine, Old Etonian, Puritan, Self Starter (Gin); Lillet Cocktail, Roy Howard, Sloe Measure (Liqueurs & Apéritifs); Culross (Rum); Wedding Bells (Whiskey – Rye); Hoots Mon (Whiskey – Scotch).

**London gin** Driest of gin styles. Leading brands include Beefeater, Gilbey, Gordon's.

**Madeira** Fortified wine of island of Madeira. Styles range from dry Sercial (the most suitable for mixing) through Verdelho and Bual to sweetest, Malmsey.

**Malibu** Popular coconut-flavoured liqueur brand. See coconut liqueur.

**Mandarine Napoléon** Cognac-based liqueur flavoured with Spanish tangerines, produced by Fourcroy of Belgium. An ingredient in Bill Gibb (Gin); Corsican Breeze, L'Aiglon, Mandarine Sour, Margarta Imperiale, Napobitter, Titanic (Liqueurs & Apéritifs).

**maraschino** Italian cherry-based sweet liqueur. Usually white, but some brands are coloured red.

**marc**   The word marc describes the pulp of skins, pips and stalks left over from the winemaking process. In several vineyard regions of France, wine producers add water to this material and distill it to make a fiery spirit also called marc. Alsace, Bourgogne and Champagne all produce marcs.

**Marnique**   Australian brandy-based liqueur. An ingredient in Asges (Gin).

**Martini**   Brand name of vermouth and sparkling-wine producer Martini & Rossi. Martini vermouths are popular for making martini cocktails, but the origins of the names are said to be unconnected.

**melon liqueur**   Spirit-based liqueur flavoured with melon. Leading brand is Japan's Midori, which has an unmistakable luminous green colour. An ingredient in Melon Balls (Liqueurs & Apéritifs); Crocodile, Melon State Balls (Vodka).

**mescal**   A Mexican relation of tequila.

**Midori**   Popular melon-flavoured liqueur. See melon liqueur.

**Noilly Prat**   Leading 'extra dry' vermouth brand of France.

**Orgeat syrup**   Almond-flavoured liquor of France.

**ouzo**   Greece's national apéritif drink, from colourless brandy or neutral spirit flavoured with aniseed. For mixing purposes, an acceptable substitute for pastis.

**Parfait Amour**   Sweet, lilac-coloured liqueur variously flavoured with almonds, citrus fruits, coriander, rose petals and vanilla. France and the United States.

**pastis**   French aniseed-flavoured liqueur and successor to absinthe. Popular brands include Pastis 51 and Ricard.

**peach schnapps**   Popular brands include Archers. An ingredient in Fluffy Navel, Woo Woo, Yikes (Liqueurs & Apéritifs), Absolute Peach, Bellinitini, Bonzai Fluff (Vodka).

**Pimm's**   Branded bitter-sweet fruit cup mix based on gin (Pimm's No. 1) or vodka (Pimm's Vodka Cup).

**pisco**   Grape brandy of Chile and Peru. Colourless.

**plum brandy**   Spirit usually from Mirabelle and Switzen plums, with their kernels. Often produced under the Germanic name of slivovitz. An ingredient of Heavenly (Brandy).

**Plymouth Gin**   England's other great gin style, besides London Dry.

**port**   Fortified wine of Portugal. For mixing, use white port or basic, inexpensive ruby and tawny ports.

**prunelle**   Liqueur flavoured with sloe kernels. An ingredient of Elk (Gin) and After Dinner (Liqueurs & Apéritifs).

**quinquina** Wine-based French apéritif with quinine flavouring. Producers include Dubonnet. An ingredient of Moonraker (Brandy), Spring (Gin), Philomel (Sherry & Madeira).

**raspberry liqueur** See crème de framboise

**rum** Dark, golden, light and 'navy' plus high-strength specialised brands. Bacardi, based in Bermuda, is the largest producer. Many recipes call for Jamaican rum, where leading dark brands include Lambs Navy, Captain Morgan and Myer's. The leading producer of white Jamaican rum is Appleton's.

**rye whiskey** Spirit distilled from a high proportion of rye mash (as distinct from other grains). Mostly United States and Canada.

**sake** Fermented rice 'wine' of Japan. In fact, closer to beer.

**Sambuca** Liquorice-flavoured Italian liqueur. Brands include Buton, Molinari. An ingredient of Via Veneto (Brandy); Matinee (Gin); Genoa, Sambuca Shooter, White Cloud (Liqueurs & Apéritifs).

**schnapps** Generic term for spirits, Germany.

**shooter** A cocktail served in a 'shot' glass. That is, a small, stemless glass with a capacity of two or three ounces. Alternative names include slammer and tooter.

**sloe gin** Liqueur gin usually home-made by steeping sloes in the spirit. Commercial producers include Gordon's. An ingredient in Millionaire, Savoy Tango (Fruit Brandies); Eclipse, Manhasset Mauler, Moll, Union Jack 2 (Gin); Alabama Slammer, Blackthorn, Charlie Chaplin, Freedom Fighter, Johnnie Mack, Love, McClelland, Moulin Rouge, Ping Pong, Shriner, Sloeberry, Sloe Gin Cocktail, Sloe Measure, Sloe Vermouth (Liqueurs & Apéritifs); Trade Winds (Rum); Sloe Teq (Tequila); Black Hawk (Whiskey – Bourbon); Border Rider, Shillelah (Whiskey – Irish).

**sour** A type of mixed drink made by shaking a spirit with sugar and lemon juice.

**Southern Comfort** Peach-flavoured, American whiskey-based liqueur made in St Louis, Missouri. An ingredient in Alabama Slammer, Helen Twelvetrees, Plantation Punch, Scarlett O'Hara, Southern Peach (Liqueurs & Apéritifs); Long Slow Comfortable Screw (Vodka); Bourbon Daisy, Comfortable Blend (Whiskey – Bourbon); Delta (Whisky – Scotch).

**Strega** Yellow-coloured herbal liqueur flavoured from 70 different plant sources. Produced at Benevento, near Naples. An ingredient in Comet, High Flyer (Gin); Calm, Grappa/Strega, Strega Flip (Liqueurs & Apéritifs); Tarantella (Rum); Vodga (Vodka).

**sugar syrup** A cocktail sweetener made simply by

dissolving sugar in a little boiling water.

**Suze**  Distinctive, gold-coloured, gentian-flavoured apéritif brand of Pernod-Ricard, France. An ingredient in Suzie (Liqueurs & Apéritifs).

**Swedish Punsch**  Sweet, aromatic prepared mixed drink of water-diluted arrack or rum with brannvin (Sweden's national grain spirit) and flavoured with wines and syrups. Traditionally drunk cold as a liqueur or mixed with boiling water, as a punch. An ingredient in Welcome Stranger (Brandy); Devonshire Pride, Diki Diki, Eve's Apple, Havana (Fruit Brandies); Biffy, CFH, Lasky (Gin); Broadway Smile, Doctor, Grand Slam, Hesitation, Hundred Per cent, Melba, Waldorf (Liqueurs & Apéritifs); Four Flush, Tanglefoot, Twelve Miles Out (Rum); Boomerang (Whiskey – Rye).

**tequila**  Mexico's national drink, distilled from a foul-tasting 'beer' called *pulque*, which is a fermentation of the succulent maguey plant.

**Tia Maria**  Leading brand (with Kahlúa) of coffee liqueur made from Jamaican rum and Jamaican Blue Mountain coffee essences, among other ingredients. Drier style than Kahlúa. An ingredient in Agadir, Black Maria, Cara Sosa, Royal Jamaican, Sombrero (Apéritifs & Liqueurs); Jamaica, Queen of Spades (Rum); Brave Bull (Tequila); Moon Landing (vodka).

**toddy**  A hot drink made from spirit mixed with lemon juice, sugar and boiling water.

**triple sec**  Drier, stronger, colourless style of curaçao. There are several Dutch brands and a well-known French one by Bardinet of Bordeaux, France. Cointreau is the best-known individual brand name. An ingredient in Betsy Ross, Bosom Caresser, Netherland (Brandy); Mandarine Sour (Liqueurs & Apéritifs); Cherie, Cuban Special, Jacqueline, Planter's Punch 2, Spanish Town (Rum); Blinding Sunrise, Chapala, Navajo Trail (Tequila); Piscy Bishop (Whisky – Scotch).

**Van der Hum**  Orange-flavoured and coloured liqueur of South Africa. Leading brand is Bertram's. An ingredient in Comet, High Flyer and Reverie (Gin) and Springbok (Liqueurs & Apéritifs).

**vermouth**  Wine-based apéritif with both its name and its flavour based in the bitter aromatic extracts of wormwood, a woody shrub. Martini & Rossi brands are best-known, and Noilly Prat is a leading dry vermouth brand.

**vodka**  Grain spirit principally of Poland, Russia and Scandinavia.

**whisky**  Spirit distilled from grains and/or malted barley. American, Canadian, Irish and Scotch whiskies describe a full range of styles.

# Index of Cocktails

299

# Acknowledgements

*Many thanks to the following people and organisations who have kindly assisted with recipes and other matters: Atlantic Bar & Grill (London), Lauren Bailey; Simon Billinghurst; Georgina Borrows; Fiona Campbell; Charles, formerly of the Hyde Park Hotel (London); Marcus Clapham; Oliver Coe; Sidwell Coe; Tim Doubleday; Corrie Ford; Robert Forester-Bennett; H. L. Delaney; Fourcroy; Tony Lord; Kevin Parker, formerly of the Lucaya Beach Hotel (Grand Bahama); Pernod-Ricard; Plymouth Gin; Mario Priester-Reading; Rainbow Room (New York); Clive Reynard; Sam Roughton; David Sandeman; Taylor, Fladgate & Yeatman; Nick White; Margaret Wood; Robin Yapp.*